Master of your Destiny

Master of your Destiny

Karma and Reincarnation explained
by Swami Sivananda
and Swami Vishnudevananda

© INTERNATIONAL SIVANANDA YOGA VEDANTA CENTRE 2025

All rights reserved. No part of this book may be reproduced or utilized in any form or by any means, electronic or mechanical, including photocopying, recording or by any information storage and retrieval system, without the prior written permission of the publisher.

The right of the International Sivananda Yoga Vedanta Center to be identified as the Author of this work has been asserted in accordance with section 14.1 of the Canadian Copyright Act.

Published by
International Sivananda Yoga Vedanta Centre
Headquarters, Sivananda Yoga Ashram
Founder: Swami Vishnudevananda
673 8th Avenue, Val Morin, Quebec, J0T 2R0 Canada
www.sivananda.org

ISBN: 978-93-48911-24-7

Also available at
MOTILAL BANARSIDASS INTERNATIONAL
41 U.A. Bungalow Road, (Back Lane) Jawahar Nagar, Delhi - 110 007
4261 (basement) Lane #3, Ansari Road, Darya Ganj, New Delhi - 110 002
203 Royapettah High Road, Mylapore, Chennai - 600 004
12/1A, 2nd Floor, Bankim Chatterjee Street, Kolkata - 700 073
Stockist: Motilal Books, Ashok Rajpath, Near Kali Mandir, Patna - 800 004

Printed & Bound by
MOTILAL BANARSIDASS INTERNATIONAL

MOTILAL BANARSIDASS
INTERNATIONAL
DELHI

Contents

Preface 1

Introduction by Marilyn Rossner, EdD, PhD 2

Swami Sivananda explains 5
   Free Will 5
   Philosophy of Right and Wrong 8
   As You Sow So Shall You Reap 11
   Man Is The Master of His Destiny 15
   Doctrine of Reincarnation 18
   Reincarnation Is Quite True 24
   Three Kinds of Karma 25
   Sin Is A Mistake Only 27
   Self-Effort versus Destiny 29
   Transmigration of Souls 31
   Theory of Rebirth 35
   Personality And Individuality 39
   Why do we not remember our past? 40
   Vedantic View of Heaven and Hell 41
   Philosophy of Death 42

Swami Vishnudevananda explains 47
   Cause and Effect 47
   Ṣamsara, the wheel of birth and death 52
   The Power of the Last Thought 55
   Karma, Rebirth and Freedom 60
   Evolution and Reincarnation 64
   Experiences of the Astral Body 66
   Lower astral entities 73
   Suicide 74

Question and Answers on Karma	**79**
With Swami Sivananda	79
With Swami Vishnudevananda	88
Stories	**95**
The Story of King Bharata and the Deer	95
A Worm speaks on the Conquest of Death	102
Rebirth – A Record of some Interesting Cases	**105**
A collection presented by Swami Sivananda	105
Tap the Source	**117**
Sivananda Yoga Vedanta Ashrams and Centres	**121**
Ashrams	121
Centres	122

Preface

The yogic teachings on karma and reincarnation can expand the understanding of life. Everyone's evolutionary development depends on what has been learned through the experiences gathered in past lives.

With this understanding one can better accept one's present circumstances and exert to improve one's situation. The teachings allow for more compassion and patience with those who struggle under difficult circumstances. And those who have elevated themselves and others through self effort inspire us to have more faith and self-confidence.

The lives of Swami Sivananda and Swami Vishnudevananda demonstrate that it is possible to be the Master of one's own Destiny. The texts which are presented in this book vibrate with this conviction.

Swami Sivananda's words have been taken from the book "Reincarnation, Karma and Disease", published by Swami Vishnudevananda in 1989.

The explanations by Swami Vishnudevananda have been extracted from lectures which were recorded in many countries, in public halls, during group meditations (satsaṅgs), in Teachers' Training Courses and symposia.

Note of Thanks

We are grateful to the many dedicated members of the Sivananda Centers who preserved and digitalized the tape recordings and created the Swami Vishnudevananda Audio Archives: **https://audioarchive.sivananda.eu/**.

We thank all those who have transcribed the audio recordings and assisted in editing the precious texts of this book.

December 2025
Sivananda Ashram Yoga Camp Headquarters,
Val Morin, Quebec, Canada

Introduction
by Marilyn Rossner, EdD, PhD

I met Swami Vishnudevananda in February 1961. From the moment I met him until today, I can say I have never met anyone more loving, more kind, more aware, more knowledgeable, more giving than Swami Vishnudevananda. I realize how blessed we are to know Swami Vishnudevanda. He introduced us to the teachings of his Master Swami Sivananda.

If we understand *karma*, we understand what is happening to us because we're all experiencing all kinds of *karma*.

Am I doing what I have come to this earth to do? Do I feel like I am fulfilling my goal, my purpose, and my mission? Am I doing what I'm supposed to do? Do I feel peaceful? What gives me meaning in life?

In a general sense, we all have the same goal, and that is to make this world a better place than how we found it.

If we understand who we really are, then it will not matter what is happening around us. I am not the body, I am not the mind, I am Satchitananda, I am existence, knowledge, and bliss absolute. I was here, I am here, I will always be here, because the soul never dies.

Ask yourself, where are the people who have died? Where are they now? Where do you think your loved ones are? They're not in heaven. They're not in hell. They are around us in what we call a spirit body or an etheric body. And they are with us, they are visiting us, and they carry on their life.

When we leave this body and go into the other world, we will see all the people we knew, and we will carry on living in the other world as a spirit.

Our soul will move on in accordance to how we have lived. We take with us into the other world every thought, every action, every hope, every place we went. We go with our character, we go with our personality, and no one can take that away. If we have been very mean and hurt people, then when the soul leaves the body, it cannot rise. It stays in the lower realms of consciousness, in the lower astral world.

If there are people around us who are talking about suicide, we always must take that seriously and try to encourage them not to commit a suicide. They don't gain anything through the suicide.

Why is there so much fear about death? The reason is that people do not know what death is. People are afraid because from one generation to another, people teach frightening ideas about death.

Heaven and hell are not places. They are states of consciousness, states of mind which we have created. If we can learn to have control over our mind, we can overcome the fear of death.

We need to take personal responsibility. We can't blame God. We can't blame our mother or father.

The world is in crisis; people are in crisis. There is so much suicide, so much emotional confusion, so many traumas and tragedies. But by understanding and practicing yoga, and by understanding reincarnation and *karma*, we can go through life more peacefully in a step-by-step fashion.

Prof. Marilyn Rossner has the gift of intuitive vision since an early age. She is a retired Professor of Special Education, Behavioral Therapist, Special Educator and Yoga Therapist. Prof. Marilyn Rossner is co-founder of the International Institute of Integral Human Sciences in Montreal, Canada.

Sri Swami Sivananda (1887-1963)

Swami Sivananda explains
Free Will

How far a man is a free agent of his actions must be intelligently understood in the light of *Vedanta*. Then only one can get a satisfactory answer and solution. In the West, various competent men have discussed this matter from various standpoints. They have not yet come to any definite conclusions. They have taken only the present into consideration. This is a sad mistake. The present is only a fragment of infinity. If the infinite past and infinite future are also taken into consideration, they will surely arrive at a definite conclusion that will bring peace and solace to the restless mind. Just as the man who has seen only one side of the shield fights with another man who has seen only the other side of the shield, so also people who know only partial truths fight amongst themselves and engage in useless controversies and debates. Just as the man who has seen the two sides of the shield can easily settle the dispute of the persons who have seen only one side of the shield, so also a *Vedantin*[1] alone, who has full knowledge of the whole truth, can settle the dispute of those people who are trying to find out whether and how far man is a free agent of his actions.

Determinists say that the will of a man is as much bound by the law of causation as the rest of the phenomena of the universe. Ethics will fall down to pieces if there is no freedom for a man. There surely cannot be any moral responsibility where there is no freedom. How could a man be made to account for his action, unless he is a free agent of his deeds? How could reward or punishment be meted out with justice to a man if he has done an action out of

---

1   A *Vedantin* is a follower or scholar of *Vedanta*, a school of Hindu philosophy that explores the nature of reality, the self, and the relationship between them.

compulsion, and not out of free choice? Man will be like an automaton or block of wood, his hands and feet being chained down tightly.

The consciousness of the Self makes a man feel that he is ever free. This idea of freedom is ingrained in the mind of every man. It is hidden in the consciousness of the Self. Though he has nothing to eat, though he is in very adverse circumstances, there is a peculiar instinct in man that prompts him to think that he is always free. Because the *nitya-mukta* (ever free) *ātman*[2] is at the back of his mind, sentiments and feelings, he feels that he is free. He knows that he is bound and that he is encased in this tabernacle of flesh. He is fully aware that he is a slave of *maya*[3] and *āvidya*[4]; and yet something inside tells him that he is free at the same time. He has this double feeling because in essence he is the all-pervading mass of wisdom (*vijnanaghana ātman*). He gets these flashes or glimpses of freedom even while he labours under straitened circumstances. There are encouragements for the struggling soul that come from within. He is in a dying condition. Doctors have pronounced the case as absolutely hopeless. Yet there is a shrill inner voice that says: "I am immortal, I am free" He cherishes an inherent feeling: "I am free though I appear to be bound. This bondage is illusory."

---

[2] *Ātman* is the spiritual life principle of the universe, especially when regarded as immanent in the individual's real self.

[3] *maya* is the illusory power that veils the true nature of reality and creates the phenomenal world as we perceive it

[4] *āvidya* is ignorance or delusion, particularly a fundamental misunderstanding of the nature of reality

Let me repeat here the words of Lord *Kriśna* in the *Bhagavad Gita*, that bespeak of the freedom of man in doing *karma*:

Ch VI, 5-6:
*uddhared ātmanā 'tmānaṁ nā 'tmānam avasādayet
ātmai 'va hy ātmano bandhur ātmai 'va ripur ātmanaḥ*
"Let a man raise himself by himself, let him not lower himself; for he alone is the friend of himself, he alone is the enemy of himself."

*bandhur ātmā 'tmanas tasya yenā 'tmai 'vā 'tmanā jitaḥ
anātmanas tu śatrutve vartetā 'tmai 'va śatruvat*
"To him who has conquered himself by himself, his own self is the friend of himself, but to him who has not (conquered) himself, his own self stands in the place of an enemy like the (external) foe."

The *Katha ūpaniṣad* also echoes the same idea:
Ch. 1.3.14:
uttiṣṭha jāgrata prāpya varān nibodhata
"Awake, arise, and, having approached a learned teacher, learn."

In conclusion I wish to point out once more that man is a free agent. He is *svatantra* or independent in doing actions. Whatever his present condition may be, he can have a glorious future through right exertion and right thinking. Many have achieved success and greatness, many have reached the goal of life through right exertion. This holds good for all. Man is ever free. May freedom be the goal of thy life! May all of us exert in the right direction to achieve freedom, the birthright of man! May that supreme Being, the *āntaryamin*[5], guide us in all our actions!

---

5 *āntaryamin* is the inner controller, the indwelling presence of the divine within all beings.

Philosophy of Right and Wrong

Right and wrong, *dharma* and *ādharma*, are both relative terms. It is very difficult to define these terms precisely. Even sages are bewildered sometimes in finding out what is right and what is wrong in some special circumstances.

That is the reason why Lord *Kriśna* says in the *Bhagavad Gita*:

Ch. IV-16, 17, 18:
kiṁ karma kim akarme 'ti kavayo 'py atra mohitāḥ
tat te karma pravakṣyāmi yaj jñātvā mokṣyase 'śubhāt
"What is action, what is inaction? Even the wise are herein perplexed. Therefore I declare to thee the action by knowing which thou shalt be liberated from evil."

karmaṇo hy api boddhavyaṁ boddhavyaṁ ca vikarmaṇaḥ
akarmaṇaś ca boddhavyaṁ gahanā karmaṇo gatiḥ
"It is needful to discriminate action, to discriminate unlawful action, and to discriminate inaction; mysterious is the path of action."

karmaṇy akarma yaḥ paśyed akarmaṇi ca karma yaḥ
sa buddhimān manuṣyeṣu sa yuktaḥ kṛtsnakarmakṛt
"He who sees inaction in action, and action in inaction, he is wise among men, he is harmonious, even while performing all actions."

I shall try to explain the terms right and wrong. *Riśi Kanada*, the author of *Vaiseśika* philosophy says in the opening *sutra*:" That which brings *niśreyasa* and *ābhyudaya* (supreme bliss and exaltation), is *dharma* (righteousness). That which elevates you and brings you nearer to God is right. That which takes you down and away from God is wrong." This is one way of defining these terms. To work in accordance with the Divine Will is right; to work in opposition to the Divine Will is wrong.

It is very difficult for the man in the street to find out what exactly the Divine Will is in certain actions. That is the reason why wise sages declare that the people should resort to *śāstras* (scriptures), learned Pandits and realized persons for consultation. A pure man who has done *niṣkāmya karma yoga* (service without personal desire) for several years and who has done worship of *īśvara* (God with form) for a long time can readily find out the Divine Will when he wants to do certain actions. He can hear the inner shrill, small voice. Ordinary people should not attempt to hear this Divine Voice, the voice of God— they may mistake the voice of the impure mind for the voice of God. The lower instinctive mind will delude them.

That work which gives elevation, joy and peace to the mind is right; that which brings depression, pain and restlessness to the mind is wrong. This is an easy way to find out right and wrong. Selfishness clouds understanding. Therefore if a man has even a tinge of selfishness he cannot detect what is right and wrong. A very pure, subtle, sharp intellect is needed for this purpose. The *Bhagavad Gita* describes the nature of *sattvic*, *rajasic* and *tamasic* natures: in chapter eighteen, verses 30 – 32 as follows:

pravṛttiṁ ca nivṛttiṁ ca kāryākārye bhayābhaye
bandhaṁ mokṣaṁ ca yā vetti buddhiḥ sā pārtha sāttvikī
"That which knows the path of work and renunciation, what ought to be done, fear and fearlessness, bondage and liberation— that intellect is *sattvic* (pure), O *Ārjuna*."

yayā dharmam adharmaṁ ca kāryaṁ cā 'kāryam eva ca
ayathāvat prajānāti buddhiḥ sā pārtha rājasī
"That by which one wrongly understands *dharma* and *adharma* and also what ought to be done and what ought not to be done— that intellect, O *Ārjuna*, is *rajasic*."

adharmaṁ dharmam iti yā manyate tamasā 'vṛtā
sarvārthān viparītāṁś ca buddhiḥ sā pārtha tāmasī
"That which, enveloped in darkness, regards *ādharma* as *dharma* and views all things in a perverted way, that intellect, O *Partha*, is *tamasic*."

Various other definitions are given by wise men to help the students in the path of righteousness. In the Bible it is said: "Do unto others as you would be done by." This is a very good maxim. The whole gist of *ṣadacara* or right conduct is found here. If one practises this very carefully, he will not commit any wrong act.

āhimsa paramo dharma – non-injury is the highest virtue. If one is well established in *āhimsa* in thought, word and deed, he can never do any wrong action. That is the reason why *Patanjali Maharīṣi* has given *āhimsa* great prominence in his *Raja Yoga* philosophy. *Ahimsa* comes first in the practice of *yama* or self-restraint. To give pleasure to others is right; to spread misery and pain to others is wrong. One can follow this in his daily conduct towards others and can evolve in the spiritual path. Do not perform any act that brings shame and fear. You will be quite safe if you follow this rule. Stick to any rule that appeals to your reason and conscience and follow it with faith and attention. You will evolve and reach the abode of eternal bliss.

Now I shall talk to you on another important point. I have already pointed out in the beginning of this chapter that 'right' and 'wrong' are relative terms. They vary according to time, special circumstances, *varna* (cast) and *aśrama* (stage of life). Morality is a changing and relative term. To kill an enemy is right for a *kṣatriya* (warrior class) king. A *brahmin* (priest) or a *ṣannyasin* (renunciate) should not kill anyone, even for protecting himself during times of danger. He should practise strict forbearance and forgiveness. To speak an untruth to save the life of a *Mahatma* (great soul) or one's *Guru* who has been unjustly charged by an unjust officer of a state is right. Untruth becomes a truth in this particular case. To speak a truth which brings harm to many is untruth only. To kill a dacoit who murders wayfarers daily is *ahimsa* only. *Himsa* becomes *ahimsa* under certain circumstances.

As You Sow So Shall You Reap

This world runs on well-established laws. There is no chaos. There is no such thing as accident or chance in life. Events occur in succession or order. There is perfect harmony. The child grows, attains boyhood and adolescence, begets children, decays and dies. The child becomes a father and the father brings forth a child. How is it that a human being is born of a human being, a horse of a horse, a cat of a cat, a dog of a dog, and a monkey of a monkey?

A seed sprouts and comes out with leaves, stems, twigs and flowers. It brings forth fruits and seeds in due seasons. A seed from this fruit brings forth a tree like the parent tree. The seed of a mango tree cannot give rise to the growth of a Jambu tree. How is it that only a mango tree comes out of a mango seed, a Jambu tree from the Jambu seed, an apple tree from an apple seed? This is a great mystery indeed. There is some mysterious power that is working behind all these phenomena. That mysterious, all-pervading power or intelligence is God. He who sows paddy reaps paddy. He who sows green gram reaps green gram. He who sows oranges reaps oranges. Man sows the seed to attain what he desires to reap. Even so, a man who does evil deeds reaps the fruits of pain. He who does virtuous actions reaps good fruits. One reaps fruits according to his Karma or actions.

How is it that one man is a king, another is a beggar, one is a genius while another is a fool, one man is very wealthy while another is in want, one is always in good health while another is constantly ailing, one is handsome while another is ugly, one man is wicked while another is a saint, one dies at the age of ten while another dies at the age of ninety? Is this due to heredity? Certainly not. The operating cause is *karma*. He who had done vicious actions in his previous birth is born as a wicked man. He who had done a lot of charity in his previous birth is born as a king. It is only the theory of *karma* that can explain things beautifully and satisfactorily.

Lord *Kriśna* says:
Bhagavad Gita, Ch. VIII-6.
yaṁ-yaṁ vā 'pi smaran bhāvaṁ tyajaty ante kalevaram
taṁ-tam evai 'ti kaunteya sadā tad bhāvabhāvitaḥ
"Whosoever at the end leaves the body, thinking of any being, to that being only does he go, O son of *Kunti*, because of his constant thought of that being."

Āvidya (ignorance), *kama* (desire), and *karma* (selfish action) are the three *granthis* or knots which bind a man to the wheel of *ṣamsara*. Man first entertains a desire to have a blanket. He says: 'Winter is very severe now. I desire to get a blanket. Then he begins to think where he can get it. He now decides to get it from the local department store. He takes the money, proceeds to the store and purchases the blanket. He had the desire at first. Then the thought made its appearance. Then there was *karma* or action of moving and purchasing. These three things, viz., the desire, the thought and the action always go together. Desire and thought are internal acts. Action is external. If a man entertains good desires, he gets good thoughts and does good actions. If a man cherishes evil desires, he develops evil thoughts and does evil actions.

It is the thought that develops the character of a man. If one cultivates thoughts of mercy, love, tolerance, generosity and understanding he exhibits these virtues in his character and behaviour towards others in society. The same rule which applies to the sowing of seeds in the soil also applies here. If one sows the virtue of mercy, he reaps a good harvest of mercy. He becomes a merciful man. If one sows cruelty, he reaps a good harvest of cruelty. He does cruel deeds. One can change one's habits, thoughts and character by developing good habits and thoughts. It is the thought that moves the body to action. There is thought behind every action. There is desire behind thought.

Do not allow desires to control your thoughts. Do not be carried away easily by all sorts of desires through emotion. When a desire manifests, cogitate, think well. Reason out whether this particular desire towards the particular object will bring maximum happiness and minimum pain. If it is otherwise, reject it ruthlessly. Do not try to fulfill it. You must control desire through thoughts. You must not allow a desire to overrule the thought. You must slowly gain the strength to control a desire. A desire, when controlled, becomes transmuted into will. You will gain will-force. Many people fall prey to their desires and are tossed about hither and thither helplessly like a straw in the wind. This is a great pity. That man who has gained control over desires and thoughts is really powerful and happy.

Learn to become wise. Learn to discriminate. Learn to control thoughts and desires. Watch your thoughts carefully. Do not allow any evil thought to enter the gates of the mental factory. Nip it in the bud. Always entertain holy, sublime thoughts and desires. Renounce unholy thoughts and unholy desires. Develop passion for Self-realization. This one strong and holy desire will annihilate all other worldly desires. Understand well the theory of *karma*. Cut the knots of *āvidya* and realize *ṣatcidananda*. Then you are beyond the operation of the law of *karma*. Then you are a *jivanmukta* or a liberated sage even while living. This is the highest goal of life. This is your highest duty. All other duties are secondary and self-imposed through *ābhimana* (pride), ignorance and delusion.

Sometimes if you are very timid, God will place you in such circumstances wherein you will be forced to exhibit courage and presence of mind by risking your life. Those world figures who have risen to eminence have utilised all opportunities to the best advantage. God shapes the minds of human beings by giving them opportunities.

Remember that in your weakness lies your real strength, because you will be always on your alert to safeguard yourself. Poverty has its own virtues. Poverty infuses humility, strength, power of endurance and the spirit of struggle and perseverance, whereas luxury begets laziness, pride, weakness, inertia and all sorts of evil habits.

Do not grumble, therefore, about bad environments. Create your own mental world and environment. That man who tries to evolve or grow in adverse environments will be a very strong man indeed. Nothing can shake him. He will be of sterner stuff. He will have strong nerves. Man is certainly not a creature of environment or circumstances. He can control and modify them by his capacities, thoughts, good actions and right exertions (*puruśartha*). *ṭhīvra* (intense) *puruśartha* can change the destiny. That is the reason why Sage *Vasiśta* in the *Yoga Vasiśta* and *Bhiśma*[6] have placed *puruśartha* above destiny. Therefore, dear brothers, exert, conquer nature and rejoice in the eternal *satcidananda ātma*.

---

6 In the *Mahabharata*, *Bhiśma* emphasizes the interplay between destiny (*daiva*) and action (*puruśartha*), highlighting that while a higher power influences events, human effort is crucial for success. He explains that *puruśartha*, the striving and actions of individuals, is essential, and *daiva* (destiny) favors those who actively pursue their goals.

Man Is The Master of His Destiny

Some ignorant people say: "*karma* does everything. It is all destiny. If l am destined by my *karma* to be like this or like that, why then should I exert? It is my destiny only." This is fatalism. This will bring inertia, stagnation and misery. This is perfect misunderstanding of the laws of *karma*. This is a fallacious argument. An intelligent man will certainly not put such a question. You have made your own destiny from within by your thoughts and actions. You have free will to choose now. You have *svatantrata* (freedom) in action. A rogue is not an eternal rogue. Put him in the company of a saint. He will change in no time. He will think and act now in a different way and will change his destiny. He will become saintly in character. *Dacoit Ratnakar* was changed into Sage *Valmiki* by the current of *Riśi Narada*.[7]

---

7 Sage *Valmiki* in his earlier life was a highway dacoit known as *Ratnakar*, who committed murder and robberies. Sage *Narada* transformed *Ratnakar* by making him repeat the name of *Rama*. However, *Ratnakar* due to his past evil tendencies could only repeat the name in reverse order, saying "Mara" (devil). But in due time the inherent power of the name of *Rama* took over the mind of *Ratnakar* who continued to repeat the name for many days, completely oblivious of his surroundings. Slowly ants built their hill around *Ratnakar* until his body was completely covered by it. When Sage *Narada* returned to see *Ratnakar*, he only saw the ant hill emanating the sound of "*Rama, Rama*..." Since then, *Ratnakar* is known as *Valmiki* or "he who emerged from an ant hill".

Jagai and *Madai*, two rogues of the first order were changed by the current of *Nityananda*, disciple of Lord *Gouranga*.[8]

You will have to desire, to think, and to act only. You can change *karma* in any way you like. You can become a *yogi* or *jnani* by right desire, by right thinking and by right action. You can attain the position of Indra (king of the heaven) or *Brahma* (creator) by good *karma*. Man is not a helpless being. He has free will of his own.

Man sows an action or thought and reaps a habit of doing or thinking. He sows a habit and reaps a character. He sows a character and reaps a destiny. Habit is second nature or rather first nature itself. Man has made his own destiny by thinking and acting. He can change his destiny. He is the master of his own destiny. There is no doubt of this. By right thinking, *vicara* (inquiry) and strong *puruśartha* (self effort) he can become master of his destiny. *Markandeya* changed his destiny through *tapas* (austerities) and worship of Lord *Śiva*.[9]

Visvamitra became a *brahmariśi* through vigorous *tapas* and changed his destiny. You can also do so, if you have strong will and iron determination. *Vasaśthaji* preaches *puruśartha* (self effort) to *Sri Rama* in the *Yoga Vasiśta*. Savitri

---

8 *Jagai* and *Madhai* were two brothers notorious for their wicked behavior during the time of *Chaitanya Mahaprabhu*. Born into a brahmin family, they indulged in drinking, meat-eating, and immoral acts, terrorizing the townspeople. One day, while Lord *Nityananda* was leading a kirtan, *Jagai* and *Madhai* attacked Him, with *Madhai* even injuring *Nityananda*'s forehead with a clay pot. However, when *Nityananda* forgave them and *Chaitanya Mahaprabhu* offered them mercy, they were transformed and became devotees.

9 *Markandeya* was a young sage destined to die at 16. He conquered death through devotion to Lord *Śiva*.

changed the destiny of her husband *Satyavan* through the power of her *pativrata dharma* (fidelity to her husband).[10]

Just as you can change your way of writing from a slant style to a vertical style, so also you can change your destiny by changing your mode of thinking. Now you are thinking: "I am Mr. So and So," identifying yourself with the body and other *upadhis* or limiting adjuncts. Now start the anti-current. Think: "I am *Brahman*. I am the immortal Self in all. I am all-pervading light, intelligence or pure consciousness." Your destiny will be changed. Just as you think, you will become. This is the *sadhana* (practice). This is the *ahamgraha-upasana* (identification with the Supreme Self). Practise it steadily. Feel and realize.

An advocate of Lahore once asked me: "*Svamiji*, you say that the law of *karma* operates with unerring precision in all men. A man desires, thinks and acts. If the actions that I perform now are the outcome of my past thoughts, and if my past thoughts are the resultant of my desires of the still more distant past, am I not helplessly bound? I am like a piece of straw tossed about hither and thither. I must act in accordance with my thought. I must think in accordance with my desire. There is no hope for my freedom of action and thinking. This does not appeal to my reason at all. Kindly throw light on this important subject."

I replied: "Look here, Mr. Dowlatram! Man is gaining new experiences and new knowledge every day. Mind is evolving every second. There is every possibility for him to change his desires, thoughts and actions. Suppose there is a thief, and he does pilfering. He removes the things of other people without their knowledge and is put into jail. People hate him. He gains many experiences. He always feels he is very miserable. He now decides to give up pilfering. He changes his desires. He now wants to lead an

---

10 The story of *Savitri* and *Satyavan*, found in the *Mahabharata*, tells of a princess who marries *Satyavan*, knowing he is destined to die within a year. *Savitri*, through her devotion and intelligence, confronts *Yama*, the god of death, and wins back *Satyavan*'s life.

honest life. His old *ṣamskaras*, his old thoughts try to resist and recur again and again. But through resolute efforts he can change his thoughts, desires and actions and can become a very good charitable man and attain perfection, freedom and immortality."

Doctrine of Reincarnation

The doctrine of reincarnation is accepted by the majority of mankind of the present day. It has been held as true by the mightiest Eastern nations. The ancient civilization of Egypt was built upon this doctrine, and it was handed over to Pythagoras, Empedocles, Plato, Virgil and Ovid, who scattered it through Greece and Italy. It is the keynote of Plato's philosophy when he says that all knowledge is reminiscence. It was wholly adopted by the Neo-Platonists like Plotinus and Proclus. The hundreds of millions of Hindus, Buddhists and Jains have made this doctrine the foundation of their philosophy, religion, government and social institutions. It was a cardinal point in the religion of the Persian Unagi. The doctrine of metempsychosis was an essential principle of the Druid faith and was impressed upon the Celts, the Gaules and the Britons. Among the Arab philosophers it was a favourite idea. The rites and ceremonies of the Romans, Druids and Hebrews expressed this faith forcibly. The Jews adopted it after the Babylonian captivity. John the Baptist was to them a second Elijah. Jesus was thought to be a reappearance of John the Baptist or one of the old prophets. The Roman Catholic purgatory seems to be a makeshift, contrived to take its place. Philosophers like Kant, Schelling and Schopenhauer have upheld this doctrine. Theologians like Julius Muller, Domer and Edward Beecher have maintained it.

Today it reigns over the Burmese, Siamese, Chinese, Japanese, Tartar, Tibetan, East Indian and Ceylonese peoples, including at least 750 millions of mankind or nearly two thirds of the human race.[11] Is it not wonderful then that this great and grand philosophical education which the Hindus, Buddhists and Jains gave the world centuries and centuries before the Christian era should or could be blotted out of existence from the Western and European world by the soul-blighting and absurd dogmas of the dark ages that supervened? By the persecution of wise men and the destruction of innumerable works in the library of Constantinople, the Church hierarchy managed to plunge the whole of Europe into mental darkness which has given the world the black record of the Inquisition and the loss of millions of human lives through religious wars and persecutions.

Here is a challenge to the non-believers of the Hindu theory of transmigration. Recently a little girl, *Santi Devi*, gave a vivid description of her past lives in Delhi. There was a great sensation in Delhi and Mathura, nay, throughout Uttar Pradesh. There was a great assembly of persons to hear her statements. She recognized her husband and child of her previous birth who are living in Mathura. She pointed out the place where money was kept, and also an old well in the house which is covered now. All her statements were duly verified and corroborated by respectable eyewitnesses. Several cases like this have occurred in Rangoon, Sitapur and various other places. They are quite common now. In such cases the Jiva takes immediate rebirth with the old astral body or linga śarira. That is the reason why memory of previous birth comes in. He does not stay in the mental world for a long time to rebuild a

---

11 An update on countries which believe in reincarnation: Countries with a significant portion of their populations believing in reincarnation include India, Sri Lanka, Kenya, Nigeria, and the Philippines, largely due to the prominence of Hinduism and Buddhism in these regions. However, belief in reincarnation is not exclusive to these countries, as it also appears in Japan, China, various African traditions like the Luo people, and in certain forms of Judaism, paganism, and some other belief systems like the Alawites and Rastafarians.

Swami Sivananda explains 19

new mind and astral body according to his previous experiences of the world.

Transmigration made its appearance in the early Christian church. Elijah was reborn as John the Baptist. "Did the blind man sin, or his parents, that he was born blind?" ask the believers in transmitted retribution. There is a period of anxiety immediately after death, when angels contend with demons for the possession of the departing soul on its way to purgatory.

Pythagoras and others obtained their belief in metempsychosis from India only. Pythagoras, who flourished in the sixth century, also taught a doctrine of transmigration, and, curiously enough, prescribed abstinence from the eating of flesh.

The suckling of a child and the act of swimming of a duckling – these instinctive acts are proofs of memory which must be the result of their corresponding and inseparable impressions left by the same acts in a previous incarnation, never mind when and where. Every act leaves *samskaras* in the *citta* (subconscious mind), which causes memory. Memory in its own turn leads to fresh actions and fresh impressions. This cycle or *cakrika* goes on from eternity like the analogy of the seed and tree.

There is no beginning for them, the desire to live being eternal, 'for them', i.e.,for the desires. Desires have no beginning or end; every being has clinging to this physical life (*ābhinivesa*). This "will to live" is eternal. Experiences are also without beginning. You cannot think of a time when this feeling of '*Aham*' or I has not existed. This I exists continuously without interruption. From this we can very easily infer that there have been previous births for us. Now, could there be fear of death to avoid pain in any being who has only been born, if he has had no experience of liability to death, it being understood that desire to avoid anything is only caused by remembrance suffered in consequence thereof? Nothing which is inherent in anything stands in need of a cause. How could it be that a child, who has not experienced this liability to death in the present life, should, as he is falling down from the mother' slap, begin to tremble and hold with his hands tightly the necklace hanging on her breast? How is it that such a child should experience the fear of death, which can only be caused by the memory of the pain consequent upon aversion to death, whose existence is conferred by the trembling of the child?

We have boy geniuses. A boy of five becomes an expert on the piano or violin. Sri *Jnanadev* wrote his commentary *"Jnaneśvari"* on the *Gita* when he was fourteen years old. There have been boy-mathematicians. There was the boy *Bhagavatar* in Madras who conducted *Kathas* (public religious speech) when he was eight years old. How could you explain these strange phenomena? They are not freaks of nature. The theory of transmigration only could explain all these things. If one man gets deep grooves in his mind by learning music or mathematics in this birth, he carries these impressions to the next birth and becomes a prodigy in these sciences even when he is a boy.

According to the Christian faith, the ultimate fate of the righteous is life eternal; of the evil, everlasting fire or eternal damnation. How could this be? No opportunity is afforded to the sinner to purify himself in later births.

The doctrine of reincarnation is common to Hinduism, Buddhism and Jainism. What is reincarnation? Reincarnation is the doctrine that the soul enters this life not as a fresh creation, but after a long course of previous existences, and will have to pass through many more before it reaches its final destination. What possible motion in the brain causes the idea 'I am I'? This recognition of a real unit does not vary from the cradle to the grave. From childhood to old age, during the whole course of the total change of all brain-molecules the idea 'I am I' is undisturbed. This 'I am I' is the soul. It is this soul which makes memory possible. It has its own consciousness and not the consciousness of anyone else, therefore it is a unit existing by itself. The law of the conservation of energy is true in the physical as well as in the spiritual world. Therefore, as no atom can be created or destroyed, so also no soul-entity can be created or destroyed. What becomes of the soul then after what we call death? No powers in the universe can annihilate it.

Reincarnation is the only doctrine which gives a complete solution to the much disputed question of original sin. There cannot be greater injustice in the world than the fact that I am now suffering for the transgression of my ancestor. Adam's responsibility for our sin is only a makeshift of the theologians. No one but the individual himself can be blamed for his wrongdoing. Are not the courts of law of the United States founded on the ideas of justice? Will any judge sitting on the throne of justice be justified in accepting the death— the voluntary suicide of Mr. B — as the proper retribution for the murder committed by Mr. A? And if he does that, will not the same judge be arraigned before a superior court, having knowingly abetted the suicide of B? And still we are asked to believe that the guilt of one man can be washed by the suffering of another.

But the doctrine of reincarnation assists most when we look at inequality and injustice and evil in the world and seek the solution. Why is one man born rich and another poor? Why is one man born among cannibals and the other in a peaceful part of the world? Why is Queen Victoria born to rule over the territories on which the sun never sets and why is a labourer in Burma to work as a slave in an Englishman's tea-garden? What is the cause of this apparent injustice? Even those who have belief in the personal creator of the universe must believe in this doctrine of reincarnation in order to exonerate God from the charge of maliciousness.

Even in the New Testament there is sufficient evidence for reincarnation. In St. John IX-2 a question is put to Jesus by his disciples: Which did sin, this man or his parents, that he was born blind? This refers to two popular theories of the time — one, that of Moses who taught that the sins of fathers would descend on children to the third and the fourth generations, and the other that of the doctrine of reincarnation. Jesus merely says that neither the man's sin nor his father's sin was the cause of his blindness; he does not deny the pre-existence of that man. Lord Jesus also says that John reincarnated as Elijah.

But people may ask if this doctrine is true, how is it that we do not remember our past incarnations. I will ask such people in what way do we exercise the faculty of memory. Certainly, so long as we are living in a body we exercise it through the brain. In passing from one incarnation to the other, the soul does not carry its former brain in the new body. Even during the course of one life, do we always remember our past doings? Can anyone remember that wonderful epoch, the infancy?

If you have knowledge of the Raja Yogic technique of perceiving the impressions directly through the process of *saṁyama* (*dhāraṇā*, *dhyāna* and *samādhi* or concentration, meditation and merging with universal consciousness at one time), you can remember your past lives. In the *Raja Yoga* philosophy of *Patanjali Mahariśi*, you will find in chapter III, verse 18:

Saṁskārasākṣātkaraṇāt pūrvajātijñānaṁ.
"By perceiving the impressions, comes the knowledge of past life."

All experiences that you have had in various births remain in the form of impressions or residual potencies in the *citta* or subconscious mind. They remain in a very, very subtle form, just as sound remains in a subtle form in a gramophone record. These subtle impressions assume the forms of waves and allow the memory of past experiences. Therefore, if a *yogi* can make a *saṁyama* on these past experiences in the *citta*, he can remember all the details of all his past lives.

Reincarnation Is Quite True

Man can hardly attain perfection in one life. He has to develop his heart, intellect and hand. He has to mould his character in a perfect manner. He has to develop various virtuous qualities such as mercy, tolerance, love, forgiveness, equal vision, courage, etc. He has to learn many lessons and experiences in this great world-school. Therefore he has to take many lives.

Reincarnation is very true. One small life is a part of the long series that stretches behind you and in front of you. It is quite insignificant. One gains a little experience only. He evolves very little. During the course of one life man does many evil actions. He does very few good actions. Very few die as good men. Christians believe that one life determines and settles everything. How could this be? How can the everlasting future of man be made to depend on that one small, little, insignificant life? If in that life he believes in Christ, he will get eternal peace in heaven; if he is an unbeliever in that life, he will get eternal damnation, he will be thrown forever into the lake of fire or into a horrible hell. Is this not the most irrational doctrine? Should he not get his chances for correction and improvement? The doctrine of reincarnation is quite rational. It gives ample chances for man's rectification and gradual evolution.

Three Kinds of Karma

Sañcita karmas are accumulated works; prarabdha karmas are ripe or fructuous actions; kriyamana or āgami karmas are current works. Sañcita is destroyed by Brahma Jnana (knowledge of the Self). One should enjoy the prarabdha anyhow (vyavaharika driśti). [12]

Kriyamana are no actions, as the jnani has akarta[13] and sakśi bhav[14]. The case in which arrows are accumulated, represents our sañcita karmas; the arrow that is ready for discharging represents our āgami karmas; and the arrow which has already left the bow, which cannot return, which must hit the target, represents the prarabdha karmas. The articles in the store-room represent the sañcita; the articles that are put in the shop for sale are prarabdha; the daily sale proceeds are the āgami.

There are three kinds of prarabdha, viz., icca prarabdha, anicca prarabdha, and paraicca prarabdha. There is difference between the icca prarabdha of vivekins (a person who has the capacity of discrimination) and non-vivekins (a person who does not apply discrimination). Non-vivekins think that they are the agents of all actions. They are egoistic. They do mischief to other people. They always do evil actions. They are always full of misery. Vivekins eradicate attachment, desires and egoism. They have no desire for money. They lead a peaceful life and serve others.

---

12 "Empirical perspective" or "worldly viewpoint". It refers to the way we perceive reality in our everyday lives, characterized by duality and change. It is the perspective of the waking state, where we experience the world as distinct entities with names and forms, engaging in actions and experiencing their consequences.

13 The feeling or attitude "I am not the doer."

14 The feeling or attitude "I am the witness or observer."

Anicca prarabdha is common to *vivekins* and *non-vivekins*. Both suffer from the heat of the sun, wind, rain, disease, accidental injury to the head by striking against the door, lightning-stroke, etc. *Paraicca prarabdha* is common to both. One man prostrates before a *vivekin* or a *non-vivekin* and implores him to render some help or service. He has to undergo the pleasure and pain that accrue from this work.

The seed-like subtle impressions of the entire accumulated action lie dormant in *cittakasa* (the mental space). When a great *jnani* gets illumination through direct intuitive knowledge, that he is not the five sheaths but transcendental to them and also their witnessing intelligence *(sakśi)*, the *ātman*, then the subtle impressions of *sancita karma* lying in *cittakasa* of the *manomaya kośa* (mental sheath of the astral body) remain in the sheath only; they can no longer enchain the liberated *jnani*.

Just as a potter, having set in motion the wheel by a rod, removes his hand and rod from it, allowing the wheel to revolve till the momentum previously imparted to it is exhausted, in the same way, the *jnani*, even after his attainment of *jivanmukti* through self-knowledge, continues enjoying the fruit of his *prarabdha karma* up to the end of the present body. *Prarabdha* is exhausted by no other means than enjoying its fruit. But they cannot produce the seed of *sancita karma* on account of his non-attachment or absence of craving for them.

The enjoyment of the fruit of *prarabdha karma* falls to his lot by the force of *prarabdha*. He has not the least desire for them as he has realized, through self knowledge, their impermanent and unreal nature. So their enjoyment does not in any way affect him. The experience of happiness and misery, owing to his non-attachment, is impotent to produce the seeds of *sancita karma*, as the parched grains are impotent to germinate and produce any crop.

Brahma Jnana annihilates *āgami karmas* (current works) of a Jnani as he has no contact with them, that is, he is untouched or unaffected by his *karmas*, like the lotus leaf which is unaffected by the drops of water on it.

The accumulated and current actions of a Jnani take shelter in *Brahmanda Prakriti*, the primordial power of the universe.

Those who serve and adore a Jnani acquire his merit of current actions, while those who hate and censure him get the demerit of his current actions.

Thus the *jnani* gets disentangled from the fetters of all *karmas (Tattwa Bodha* – a scripture by *Sri Śankaracarya).*

Sin Is A Mistake Only

Only the ignorant man says: "I am a great sinner." This is a serious mistake. Never for a moment think that you are a sinner. You are the most holy one, you are the ever-pure *ātman.* Sin cannot touch you. You are above vice and virtue, *dharma* and *ādharma. Punya* and *Papa*, merit and sin, are mental creations only. Sins are mistakes only. An ignorant *jiva* (individual soul) commits these mistakes during the course of his journey in this world on account of *āvidya* or ignorance. Through mistakes he gains experiences and marches forward in his path of spirituality. Every mistake is your best teacher. One has to evolve through sins and mistakes. These mistakes are inevitable. Some people become a prey to thoughts of sin. They ever brood: "We are great sinners. We have committed many crimes." This is a great blunder.

Whenever thoughts of this nature worry you, you should think: "I am doing Japa of *Om*. This will burn all old sinful actions. This will purify my mind. I am doing *tapas,* fasting and charity. These are all great purifiers. I am becoming purer and purer. Nothing can affect me now. I am like the effulgent fire. I have become a holy person." Assert, whenever such negative thoughts of sin trouble you: "I am the *nitya sudha,* ever-pure *ātman.*"

Hear the words of assurance of Lord Krishna in the *Bhagavad Gita*, Ch. IV-36, 37, 38:

api ced asi pāpebhyaḥ sarvebhyaḥ pāpakṛttamaḥ
sarvaṁ jñāna plavenai ' va vṛjinaṁ saṁtariṣyasi
"Even if thou art the most sinful of all sinners, yet shalt thou cross over all sin by the raft of wisdom."

yathai 'dhāṁsi samiddho 'gnir bhasmasāt kurute'rjuna
jñānāgniḥ sarva karmāṇi bhasmasāt kurute tathā
"As the burning fire reduces fuel to ashes, O *Ārjuna*, so doth the fire of wisdom reduce all action to ashes."

na hi jñānena sadṛśaṁ pavitram iha vidyate
tat svayaṁ yogasaṁsiddhah kālenā 'tmani vindati
"Verily, there is no purifier in this world like wisdom; he that is perfected in *yoga* finds it in the Self in due season."

And *Bhagavad Gita* Ch. IX - 30, 31, 34:

api cet sudurācāro bhajate māṁ ananyabhāk
sādhur eva sa mantavyaḥ samyag vyavasito hi saḥ
"Even if the most sinful worships Me with undivided heart, he too must be accounted righteous, for he hath rightly resolved."

kṣipraṁ bhavati dharmātmā śaśvacchāntiṁ nigacchati
kaunteya pratijānīhi na me bhaktaḥ pranaśyati
"Speedily he becometh dutiful and goeth to eternal peace. O *Kaunteya*, know thou for certain that My devotee perisheth never."

manmanā bhava madbhakto madyājī māṁ namaskuru
mām evai 'ṣyasi yuktvai 'vam ātmānaṁ matparāyaṇaḥ
"Fix the mind on Me, be devoted to Me, sacrifice unto Me, bow down to Me, having thus united thy whole self in Me, taking Me as the supreme goal, thou shalt come to Me."

Self-Effort (Purushartha) versus Destiny (Prarabdha)

One philosopher says: "It is very difficult to say how *puruśartha* brings results and how it operates." Another philosopher says: "Everything is prearranged in the grand plan or grand scheme. God knows the whole details of evolution of a man from mineral life till he becomes a Jivanmukta or liberated soul. In reality all is *prarabdha* only. We will have to preach *puruśartha* just to give an impetus to the man to work in right earnest. Otherwise he will become slothful and dull."

The man who advocates the theory of *puruśartha* says: "Am I a straw to be tossed about hither and thither? I can change my *prarabdha*. I will undo it by *vedantic* practice. I have free will of my own. I will make it pure and irresistible. I will work out my salvation. I will become free myself."

No one can remain quiet even for a second. No one can become a fatalist. There is an urge or stimulus from within to work. That is the reason why the *Gita* says in Chapter III, 5:

na hi kaścit kṣaṇam api jātu tiṣṭhaty akarmakṛt
kāryate hy avaśaḥ karma sarvaḥ prakṛtijair guṇaiḥ
"Nor can anyone even for an instant remain actionless; for helplessly is everyone driven to action by the qualities born of nature."

The theory of *prarabdha* cannot make anyone a fatalist. For a Bhakta it is all *prarabdha* only; for he is a man of self-surrender. He has to glorify the power of the Lord. For a Vedantin it is all *puruśartha*; for he is a man of self reliance. He has to glorify the power of his own strong will (Atma Bala). Both are correct from their own viewpoints.

Prarabdha is only *puruśartha* of previous births. God and *puruśartha* are synonymous terms. They are two names for one thing. Trial or luck, *puruśartha* or *prarabdha*, free will or necessity,—all these are synonymous terms. If a man succeeds in his attempt he calls it *puruśartha*. He says: "I really exerted much. I have succeeded." If he fails the same man says: "What can I do, my friend? It is all *prarabdha*. Without Him nothing can be done. Without God not an atom can move, no leaf can wave in the air." In the *Mahabharata* you will find that exertion and *prarabdha* combined bring about fruits. If you are ailing, you must do *puruśartha*. You must take medicine. You should leave the results to *prarabdha*.

Throughout the Yoga Vasishtha, *Sri Vasiśtaji* recommends only *puruśartha* to *Sri Rama*. Through *puruśartha*, *Markandeya* conquered death. Man is doubtless the master of his destiny. What is destiny after all? It is one's own makeup. You have created certain things. You can destroy them or undo them also. You are thinking in one way now: "I am Mr. So and So. I am a *brahmin*. I am a doctor. I am stout. I am a householder." This is *prarabdha*. You can change this particular mode of thinking. Think: "I am Brahman. I am omnipotent. I am the witness or *sakśi*. I am God. I am neither body nor the mind. I am the all-pervading Truth or pure consciousness." This is *puruśartha*.

Transmigration of Souls

The word 'transmigration' means passing from one life to another. The one great and fundamental tenet of most schools of Indian Philosophy, with the exception of the Charvaka or the materialist, is the belief in the immortality of the soul. The soul passes through a number of lives for attaining perfection. This is technically called 'transmigration of souls.'

Belief in the metempsychosis or transmigration of souls dates from primeval times. It is as early as primitive man. One solution to the mystery of death, and a consoling thought about death, is the indestructibility of the soul and its existence after death in other forms.

The purpose of transmigration is not reward or punishment, but betterment and perfection. It prepares the human being for the ultimate realization which frees him from the cycle of births and deaths. It is not possible to achieve perfection and absolute freedom without a plurality of lives.

Man develops tendency and aptitude in several births and becomes a genius in one birth. Buddha gained experiences in several births. He became a Buddha only in his last birth. In one birth all virtues cannot be developed. One can cultivate the virtues by gradual evolution. The baby sucks, the young duck swims. Who taught this? They are the *samskaras* or the tendencies of previous births.

There had been many instances of children like Santi Devi, etc. who have narrated all about their previous lives. All these have been fully corroborated also. The children have actually pointed out the houses in which they lived in their previous lives.

Soul, retribution, transmigration, divinity were all accepted by Plato. Pythagoras also taught the doctrine of transmigration. *Buddha* also taught the doctrine of transmigration.

The older Egyptians embalmed their dead and buried them in the best tombs they could afford. The deceased had a kind of twin soul, one half of which remained in the tomb as long as the body continued undecayed, while the other proceeded on passport (applied for the journey) to the immortal gods. The requisite indication was given by a divine Judge, whose opinion as to destiny was final. Transmigration in some obscure form was thus held by Egyptian priesthood.

The human body is only a vesture and dwelling place for the human soul. The soul can certainly re-inhabit another dwelling place and put on another vesture in order to develop and realize better than before the Divine plan and purpose for it. The Creator has so planned. The soul of a depraved and corrupted human being is given another training in another body. The evolution of all beings is for a better condition. Evolution to the higher and not deterioration to the lower is generally the law and principle of nature. But there is exception to the general rule.

The soul armed with little virtue and divinity gained in the previous existence enters another life to increase, develop and better that original stock. There is no greater response of the body controlled by the soul to God, Goodness, Truth, Holiness and other attributes of God.

No opportunity is afforded to the sinner to purify himself in later births. His finite sin, if not somehow purged, precipitates him at death into endless misery. This cannot be. This is not reasonable. The doctrine of transmigration gives ample scope for the sinner to correct and educate himself in future births. Vedanta says that there is hope of salvation even for the worst sinner.

He reaps the harvest of his misdeeds for a limited period. After he has been purged of his sins, he is again born as a rational being and is thus given a fresh chance for working out his emancipation, with freedom of will to choose the right path or the wrong one, and with the knowledge to distinguish the one from the other.

You are responsible for your well-being or otherwise, through your own *karma* or action. The diversity in individual characters, the different predilections or tendencies of the different children at their births and the inequalities of human lives can only be accounted for and explained through the Law of *Karma*. The Law of *Karma* gives liberty and freedom to an individual to grow to his full perfection.

The image of man is reflected in a mirror. Nothing passes from the man to the image. The image is not the same as the man nor yet is it another. In exactly the same way rebirth takes place. The new being is like the image. The Karma which gives rise to the new being is like the mirror, through the agency of which the image of the man is reflected.

The enlightening influences of yogis and sages, their lives and teachings assert themselves more and more in the new life. The light of God is more sought after and the gravitation towards God becomes stronger and stronger. More and more the life gets fitted to see God and hear His voice. Progress advances from one existence to the next — we cannot say through how many lives — until the final and stainless state of perfection is reached and the individual soul merges itself in the Supreme Soul.

Whence have I come? Whither shall I go? These questions will be asked by every intelligent person. They are the problems of life. Your present life is but one in a series of countless incarnations, though all are not necessarily in the human form.

The union of the soul with a particular body is known as birth and its separation therefrom is called death. When the soul leaves its physical sheath, it transmigrates into another body, human, animal or even vegetable, according to its merits. The *Kathopaniṣad* says:"Now I will tell you, O *Naciketas*, the eternal and divine mystery as to how the soul fares after attaining death. Some souls attain to other bodies, while some fall to the vegetable state, according to their action and knowledge" (1-1-18).

The process of transmigration continues till the soul, purged of all its impurities, and having acquired a true and full knowledge of the Imperishable Soul by *yoga*, attains *mukti* or the final emancipation and enjoys perfect, eternal bliss by its union with the Supreme Self or *para brahman*.

According to Indian philosophy, there is a subtle body, or *sukṣma śarira* within the physical body. When the physical body perishes, this subtle body does not perish. It moves to heaven to enjoy the fruits of its good actions done here. This subtle body perishes only when the soul attains final emancipation. The impressions or *ṣamskaras*, the tendencies or *vasanas*, are carried in the subtle body.

There are blessed souls like *Vama Deva, Jnana Dev, Dattatreya, Aṣtavakra* and *Ṣankaracarya*, who in their very first entry into the world attained a high degree of perfection before death. They are all born *ṣiddhas*. Most souls will need further rebirths for their full perfection and attainment of *mokśa*.

A good soul makes a good body, a bad soul a bad body. The body is an indispensable aid to the soul in its progress towards God. The body was designed by God to carry the soul on its onward march. Petrol and steam are great forces. But by themselves they cannot make the journey with a definite course and a definite destination. They must be harnessed to a machine, a running train or steamer. A pilot or a driver puts petrol or steam into the conveyance and drives and steers it toward his destination. Therefore, the soul must have a body to run its course and reach its destination in God.

When knowledge of the Imperishable is attained, there is no more transmigration. Mother *Prakriti*'s (nature) work is over now. She shows all the experiences of this world to the individual soul and takes him higher and higher through various bodies till he gains back his essential divine nature.

Theory of Rebirth

Man can be compared to a plant. He grows and flourishes like a plant and dies in the end, but not completely. The plant also grows and flourishes and dies in the end. It leaves behind it the seed which produces a new plant. Man leaves when dying his *karma* behind— the good and bad actions of his life. The physical body may die and disintegrate, but the impressions of his actions do not die. He has to take birth again to enjoy the fruits of these actions. No life can be the first, for it is the fruit of previous actions; nor the last, for its actions must be expiated in the next life following. Therefore, *ṣamsara* or phenomenal existence is without beginning or end. But there is no *ṣamsara* for a *jivanmukta*, or liberated sage, who is resting in his own *ṣat-chit-ānanda ṣvarupa* (essence of existence absolute, knowledge absolute and bliss absolute).

When a man dies he carries with him the permanent *linga śarira* or astral body, which is made up of
- 5 *jnana indriyas* or sense organs or organs of knowledge: eyes (sight), ears (sound), nose (smell), tongue (taste), and skin (touch)
- 5 *karma indriyas* sense organs or organs of action: mouth, hands, feet, anus, and genitals
- 5 vital energies: *prāṇa, apāna, samāna, udāna, vyāna*
- 4 components of the mind:
  Manas (mind) – thinks and doubts
  Citta (subconscious) – storehouse of memories
  Buddhi (intellect)
  Ahaṅkara (ego), the self-assertive principle

and the changing *karmasraya* (receptacle of works), the actions of the soul, which determines the formation of the next life.

Sri *Jnanadev*, the reputed Yogi of Alandi, wrote his commentary on the Gita, *"Jnaneśvari"*, when he was only sixteen years old. He was a born *siddha* (perfected soul). You can also become a Siddha if you try in right earnest. What one has attained can be achieved by another also.

If a new-born child who has not done any wrong action in this birth undergoes great suffering, this is the fruit of some evil deed done in previous birth. If you ask how the person was induced to do a wrong action in his former birth, the answer is that it was the result of some action done in a birth still anterior and so on.

Many intelligent fathers have sons with dull intellect. If a shepherd boy gave you some food and water in your previous birth when you were dying of starvation, he will be born in this birth as your son, with a dull intellect to enjoy your property.

When creatures are born, they evince a desire to suck the breast and show an instinct of terror. Therefore, it follows that they remember the sucking of the breast and pains experienced in the previous birth. This shows that there is rebirth.

Even a child exhibits *harsha* (exhilaration), *soka* (grief), fear, anger, pleasure and pain. The *dharm-ādharma ṣamskaras* (impressions of right and wrong) of this birth cannot be the cause of theses. The *ṣamskaras* of the previous birth must have a support (*asraya*). From this we can clearly infer the existence of the *jiva* (individual soul) in the previous birth, and the *jiva* is *ānadi*, or beginningless. If you do not accept that the *jiva* is *ānadi*, the two defects, viz., *kritanasa* and *ākritabhyagama* will creep in. Pleasure and pain which are the fruits of virtuous and vicious actions done previously will pass away without being enjoyed. This is *kritanasa* (loss of merited reward). So also, one will have to enjoy the pleasure and pain, the fruits of good and evil actions, which are not done by him previously. This is *ākritabhyagama* (receiving unmerited reward). In order to get rid of these two defects we will have to accept that the *jiva* is *ānadi* or beginningless. Else, life would be unaccountable.

Some Yogic students ask me: "How long should one practise *śirśasana* (headstand) or *pascimottanasana* (forward bend) or *khumbhaka* (breath retention) or *mahamudra* (a special asana), to awaken the Kundalini? Nothing is mentioned on this point in any book on *Yoga*." A student starts his *sadhana* from the point or stage he left in his previous birth. That is the reason why Lord *Kriśna* says to *Arjuna* in the *Bhagavad Gita* in Ch VI- 42,43:

athavā yoginām eva kule bhavati dhīmatām
etadd hi durlabhataram loke janma yad idṛśam
"Or he may be born in a family of wise *yogins*. A birth like this is verily very difficult to obtain in this world."

tatra tam buddhi samyogam labhate paurva dehikam
yatate ca tato bhūyaḥ samsiddhau kuru nandana
"There he recovereth the characteristics belonging to his former body and with these he again laboureth for perfection, O Joy of the Kurus."

It all depends upon the degree of purity, stage of evolution, the degree of purification of the *nadis* (energy channels) and the *pranamaya kośa* (vital sheath), degree of *vairagya* (non-attachment) and yearning for liberation.

Some are born with purity and other requisites of realization on account of their having undergone the necessary discipline in their past life. They are born *siddhas*. *Guru Nanak, Jnana Dev, Varna Deva, Aśtavakra* were all adepts from their very boyhood. *Guru Nanak* asked his teacher when he was a boy, about the significance of OM. *Varna Deva* delivered a lecture on Vedanta when he was dwelling in his mother's womb.

Man does actions with the expectation of getting fruits, and so he takes a birth to enjoy the fruits of his actions. In the next birth, he does some more actions and he has to take another birth. In this manner the *samsaric* wheel is revolving from eternity to eternity. When one gets knowledge of the Self, he is liberated from this round of births and deaths. *Karma* is beginningless and *samara* is also beginningless. When a man does actions without expectation of fruits in selfless spirit, all fetters of *karma* get loosened gradually.

Die to live. Kill this little 'I' and attain immortality. Live in *brahman*. You will live forever. Possess *ātman*. You will have eternal life. Identify with your soul. You will cross the ocean of death, or *ṣamsara*. Rest in your *ṣatcidananda ṣvarupa* (the essence of existence absolute, knowledge absolute and bliss absolute). You will have eternal life.

A leech moves on a blade of grass and reaches the end of the blade. It first catches hold of another blade with the forepart of its body and then draws its hind part onto it. Even so, the *jivātman* (individual soul) abandons the present body at the time of death, fashions the future body by his thought and then enters that body.

A good or bad deed always brings its good and bad fruits. You will find in the *Mahabharata*:

Yadrisham kriyate karma tadrisham bhujatephalam
Yadrisham vapyate bijam tadrisham prapyate phalam
"Just as a calf finds its mother among a thousand cows, so also an action that was performed in a previous birth follows the doer."

Just as the fruit corresponds to the seed that has been sown, so also the fruit of the actions that are performed by us corresponds to the nature of the actions we perform. This is an infallible law of nature. He who has sown the seed of a mango tree cannot expect a jack fruit. He who has done evil actions throughout his life, cannot expect happiness, peace and prosperity in his next life.

Many are the times we have all been together in the past and also been separated and so again shall it be in the future. Even as a heap of grain removed from the granary ever assumes new order or arrangement and new combination, so is the case with the *jiva* (human being) in the universe through this arrangement. (*Yoga Vaśista*).

Personality And Individuality

There is a distinction between personality and individuality. Many have no clear understanding of these two terms. They get these mixed up and are confused. Some people think that personality is individuality and individuality is personality. That which distinguishes a person from a thing or one person from another is personality. Personality in common parlance refers to the body. When a man is tall, has good complexion and beautiful features, when his face has a fine cut, we say that Mr. So-and-so has a charming personality. When one is able to influence others, people say that such-and-such a man has strong personality. When one is timid and shy we say that such and such a man has weak personality; he must develop his personality. Personality counts much in society for success in life.

The term personality comes from the Latin *persona*, the mask. Personality is that particular consciousness which concerns the physical body. Mr. or Mrs. or Miss So and so is the personality. Hunger, thirst, physical beauty, black or red colour, height, stature, anger and all the limitations of the body relate to the personality. He is a *brahmin*. He is a *sannyasin*. He is a merchant. He is a doctor. All these concern the personality. This is the mask which the man is putting on now.

Death destroys the personality, but it cannot annihilate the individuality. Individuality is separate and has distinct existence. It is something which is beyond the body. It has no relation to your personality at all. It is the sense of 'I'. It is like a continuous current. It is the continuity of the one thought, the thought of 'I'. All other thoughts are centred round this 'I'. I was a boy. I become a man. I was a doctor. I ate. I drank. I spoke. I meditated. I talked. I went to America, England, France and Germany. The same 'I' has gone through all these experiences. 'I' is the dweller in this body. 'I' is the same in childhood, youth and old age.

Personality changes but your individuality, the sense of 'I' can never change because the sense of 'I' will continue to exist with you. After leaving this physical body the sense of 'I' continues to exist. After death you take the sense of 'I' with you. Even in dream you have the sense of 'I' within. Even in deep sleep you have the sense of 'I'. If you have not got the sense of 'I' in deep sleep, you would not remember that you slept happily.

You can lose this individuality by becoming one with the Supreme Self or *para brahman* through meditation and *nirvikalpa samadhi*. Just as the water in the pot becomes one with the ocean when the pot is broken, so also the individuality becomes one with the Infinity or the Universality when ignorance is destroyed, when the idea of separateness is annihilated through knowledge of the Imperishable or *brahma jnana*. Do you see now clearly the difference between personality and individuality?

Why do we not remember our past?

An objection is brought against the doctrine of reincarnation. That objection is, "Why do we not remember our past?" Do you remember what you did in your childhood? Will you say you did not exist then, because you cannot remember? Certainly not. If your existence depends upon your memory then this argument proves that you did not exist as child, because you do not remember your childhood. The details have passed out of your memory, but the knowledge you have acquired through your experiences is still in your subconscious mind or Chitta as impressions.

If you remember your past, you may make a bad use of the present. Your inveterate enemy in your past life may be born as your son in this life. If you remember the past, you will draw your sword to kill him. Feelings of enmity will rise in your heart at once. When you enter college, you carry with you all the knowledge you acquired at school. You increase and develop that kind of knowledge in your higher studies. You do not remember fully everything you did at school, yet the experience is there when you are in college. Even so past experience influences your present life.

Mother Nature has concealed the past from you. It is not desirable to remember the past. Suppose for a moment you know the past—you know that you have committed a sinful action in your past life and you are going to suffer for it. You will be thinking of this always. You will worry yourself constantly. You will not have sound sleep. You will not relish your food. That is the reason

Vedantic View of Heaven and Hell

According to *Vedanta,* heaven and hell are certain degrees of consciousness, they are not entirely 'outside'. The joys of heaven are spoken of only to persuade the virtuous to greater deeds of virtue, goodness, love and service. The torments of hell are presented only to dissuade the wicked people from their wicked, unrighteous, evil, harmful deeds.

By purity, goodness, love, service, the human mind forms around itself, its own heaven; by impurity, error, evil, ignorance, the human mind creates for itself suffering and sorrow that go by the name of hell. It is true, as poet Milton sang, mind in its own place can in itself make a heaven or a hell.

Man is, in his true and essential inner spiritual nature, eternal, unborn, infinite, of the nature of light, joy, peace. It is ignorance that is the root-cause of his suffering, limitations, individuality, error, birth and death. Self-realisation, the experience of the Infinite Self within himself, releases man into the Kingdom of Infinite Peace, Freedom and Bliss.

That there is an independent plane of existence called hell, subsisting in its own right, is fully supported by the *puranic* literature. Suppose there is a wicked and inveterate drunkard given over to insensibility of every type and vice.

After death he is led by the messengers of death to that plane of existence called hell, and left to suffer the torments of a tantalus, the tortures of moving in scorching deserts where his agonising thirst for drink is not quenched. Thus in suffering he is made to pay back the wages of his error and purify his soul. Similarly, there is an independent plane of existence called heaven to which the virtuous are led.

Philosophy of Death

Occasionally in moments of calm contemplation, when we are thrown in an introspective mood, we sometimes wonder why God, who is such a kind, compassionate and merciful Father, should have included death in the scheme of life. The fact is, death comes as a necessity to egg us on in our evolution.

Could you just imagine of a world where there would be no death? Over population even today poses as a difficult problem with all the deaths that are taking place in normal course. So, imagine the extent of chaos and confusion that would result if there would be no deaths. Life would no longer be worth living. It would become a dull drab drudgery.

Living in the same body we cannot grow beyond our bonds and ties of attachments. Complete separation is necessary to make us cautious of our attachments. During our brief sojourn in this world, we get so much attached to this *terra firma* that when death knocks at our door, we feel too reluctant to be torn from our family surroundings and leave our material possessions so painstakingly created.

Therefore, to completely snap the tie of attachment, death is the only solution.

Death is not only a necessity for those who die, but it is also necessary for the evolution of those who are left behind. Death helps devolve responsibilities on new shoulders. They accept the challenge of life and grow in experience. Father suddenly passes away. Son takes up the new responsibility, bears it and enriches his treasure-house of experience. When a child dies in his infancy, it may not be much of an assimilation of experience for him except for certain *karmic* purgation, but it means all the more for those who are left behind. We have to grow beyond attachment, ego and desire to enjoy immunity from sufferings. Thus, by helping us transcend our worldly attachments, death plays an indispensable role.

In fact, an individual soul could never grow without death. The evolutionary process is a long one. It requires various types of experiences of poverty and riches, of purity and pollution, of ignorance and education of every country, clime, culture, race and religion. It requires experiences of both the sexes as well. In a single body all this is not possible to assimilate. Therefore, by virtue of necessity we die and are born again under different circumstances for a different set of experiences.

Assimilation of experiences is also not possible without death. In the post-mortem states the consciousness widens. The deeds of the past lifetime have a reaction, and we learn many new lessons. We often notice monkeys devouring eatables rapidly and then masticating them at leisure. Similarly, we masticate our experiences in a higher and wider light which shines after death. During our stay in the astral plane, the scenes of our past life flit pass our eyes one after another. We begin to relive our lives with the difference that now we are identified with all the actors in every situation. We feel as we did, when we tortured someone as also like the one who was tortured by us. We experience the pain of the latter. This process exhausts our *karma* to a degree and provides us a useful lesson. *Karmic* purgation occurs when both, the oppressor and also the oppressed have been able to excuse each other. Retaliation only augments *karmic* bondage.

Death comes as a necessary drop-scene between two births. It is a drop-scene inasmuch as the activities go on behind the curtain. Thus, after the assimilation of one set of experiences of one life, the individual soul is provided again with a new set of mental, emotional and pranic body, eminently suited for his next reincarnation. In this manner from life to life, he travels assimilating his diverse experiences.

In normal course, the period that intervenes between two births is about four to five hundred years (in occult parlance our one year is equal to one day of *pitris* or ancestors). But occasionally instances are there which indicate that births have been immediate. Invariably in all such cases where the births have been immediate, the death has been in an accident. Where we have not completed the experiences of one birth up-to-date, a second birth in similar surroundings for similar experiences, becomes absolutely necessary. The other reason is that sometimes the attachments and certain resolutions are so overwhelmingly overpowering that in order to exhaust them a second birth in the immediate future becomes absolutely necessary. For illustrations we need not go to the distant past. Narrations of a young girl, *Mridula* from *Dehra Dun*, who came to meet me in 1960, corroborate the validity of my statement. But it may be remembered that in all such cases the memory of the previous birth does not last long. Sometimes, instances have also been found where the dead man has come back to life. Sri Chandresekhara Iyer of Hyderabad, Deccan, who was a resident in Śivanandashram was an example, who died, and after being dead for two hours, came back to life and lived for some time afterwards.

At the time of death, a little distortion and contraction which we find in the body is just the effort of the pranic double to extricate itself from the physical body. The experience is said to be painless. But how does it matter even if it were painful when death promises light behind the curtain!

Sri Swami Vishnudevananda (1927 – 1993)

Swami Vishnudevananda explains
Cause and Effect

Karma or the actions we perform consist of three categories: *sattvic, rajasic* and *tamasic*. *Sattvic karma* is the action performed with a pure mind, without expecting anything in return. *Rajasic karma* is done for a specific purpose, to obtain specific results. *Tamasic karma* is performed without a specific purpose, it clouds your thinking and brings pain to yourself as well as to others.

Sattvic action leads you upwards, *rajasic* action holds you in the middle, and *tamasic* action leads you downwards into a lower birth.

But even the most *sattvic* action can bind you to the result. *Karma Yoga* teaches how to escape from all reactions whether *sattvic, rajasic* or *tamasic*.

There is no action which is absolutely *sattvic, rajasic* or *tamasic*. It can be predominately *sattvic* mixed with *rajas* and *tamas*, or predominantly *rajasic* mixed with *sattva* and *tamas*, or predominantly *tamasic* mixed with *sattva* and *rajas*.

Any action which is performed consciously, knowingly and willfully will have its reaction. This is also stated in the law of physics which says that every action has a similar and opposite reaction. It also applies to the energy with which we perform an action.

Every action of the physical body begins in the mind, at the thought level. From there it moves into the physical body. The physical action corresponds to a thought which originated in the mind.

The word *karma* has a twofold meaning: it refers both to the action and the reaction. If you see a tree, you know there must be a cause for the tree. Though you cannot see the cause, you know there must be a seed, from which the tree originated. The cause is the seed, and the effect is the tree.

At the same time, the effect which is called the tree also contains the cause. The tree itself is the cause for further seeds.

The apple tree came from an invisible apple seed. That seed has disappeared, but you see the effect in the form of many apples growing on the tree which contains the seeds.

This is an example of how the effect is in the cause and the cause is in the effect. They are interrelated. You cannot separate one from another.

Cause and effect are interwoven. The practice of *karma yoga* teaches how to dissolve both cause and effect.

Your physical body has a deep cause. You did not materialize simply from nowhere because of your parents. Even if your parents were not born, still the effect of your birth would have come through other parents.

There must be a cause for your body beyond your parents. This is called *karma*. Because of certain desires and actions which you performed in the past, the seed of your present birth was created in the past, maybe in several past lives. One effect of these seeds is taking effect now in the form of the Yoga Teachers Training Course.

In the history of the west, there was never such a thing as a yoga vacation or our present Yoga Camp. It appears to be new, but there is also a cause for this: I was doing this in my past lives and was not satisfied. Therefore, I must continue where I left. The effect of my *karma* made me clear the land for this camp and to continue teaching the techniques where I had left them in a past life. And at the right time you were born. And as you grew up, your *yoga karma* is now materializing as an effect. It is not because of me; it is an effect which is manifesting.

What you are experiencing now is the effect; the cause is far behind you. Generally, we cannot see the cause, we see only the effect. You see the apple tree with beautiful, sweet apples. They are the effect. But you cannot see the seed, or the man who planted the seed. The farmer who planted the seed is dead and gone. The originator of the seed has disappeared; you see only the effect. We forget the cause.

But anything that happens in this world – a war, a tornado, a terrorist attack, is both an individual as well as a collective *karma* or effect. Even if you are doing a positive action now, the good action's effect may not be manifesting immediately. There can even be a negative reaction.

Today, the Greenpeace ship "Rainbow Warrior" which was going from New Zealand to protest against the French nuclear blast somewhere in the Pacific, was destroyed by an explosion in a New Zealand harbor. The ship sank, and a Portuguese photographer, who was a member of this mission, died. Even though their mission was a peaceful protest, the effect was not peaceful.

Mahatma Gandhi preached and practiced non-violence. He lived a simple mendicant's life. He was involved in Indian politics, the Independence movement to free India from the British rule. He organized many satyagraha ("holding firmly to truth") events of peaceful disobedience. Once India obtained its independence, he did not take on any political role, while others like Nehru became prime minister and took other government posts. Gandhi could have been prime minister or president, but he did not want this. He just continued to wear a dhoti or loin cloth and lived a simple life in an ashram. He conducted prayer meetings. He ate simple vegetarian food. He continued to preach non-violence and truthfulness. He did not accept any power or position. Gandhi preached unity between Hindus and Muslims and other religions. Yet he was shot by a fanatic Hindu. That was the effect.

We cannot see the cause for this, because he did not do anything wrong in this life. He preached only non-violence. He lived a truthful life, a simple life even after India attained independence. But there must be a cause for this.

Just because we cannot see the immediate cause, this does not mean it happened haphazardly. That is the problem with our reasoning. Why was Mahatma Ghandi shot? He was not a person like a pope with positions and power, under constant political pressure from bishops and cardinals. The pope is actually like a prisoner, even though he is called pope. But Mahatma Ghandi was not a prisoner; he knew that politics, power, position and money would increase his ego. He abandoned all these like a great Indian yogi saint. Therefore, it seems that there was no cause why he was shot. Especially why he was shot by someone of his own religion. It was a Hindu who shot him, not a Muslim. How can this be explained?

Generally, we cannot see the cause. The cause might be coming from this life or from the past. Some of the causes may be taking effect now, but other causes may remain inactive. Like seeds lying in cookie jar may sprout only thousands of years from now. Some of the actions which you are performing now may not materialize in this life, but only in future lives.

All the seeds of *karma* cannot be sown in the same field. Imagine that a farmer has a field of five acres. He has sown and harvested wheat on the field. But he cannot sow all that harvested wheat again on the same five acres. When the farmer harvested the wheat, a certain portion was reserved as seeds to be sown for the next season, and the remaining part was stored for the daily bread of the farmer. And a third part remained stored as an emergency reserve, in case the next harvest goes bad due to lack of rain.

The same process goes on in the karma of our life. The karma which you have sown in the past is too much to handle in one life, in one body. There are so many varieties of *karmas* which you have sown: *sattvic, rajasic* and *tamasic karmas*. We cannot enjoy or suffer all of them at once, our body cannot take that. So from that granary certain *karmas* are taken for your daily bread, which you are now enjoying. That is called *prarabdha karma. Prarabdha* is the effect which can now be seen. You are born in a good family which is spiritual, yogic or religious. Or you may be born in a poor drug addicted family where the children are born drug addicts because of the drug abuse of their parents.

Why is one baby suffering while another baby is born in a palace? We cannot see the cause, but from the analogy of the tree we understand that there must be a cause. The cause is exactly what the effect is, and the effect is exactly what the cause is.

The newborn baby who is having a drug addiction problem from its very birth, started that cause in previous lives; he could have been selling drugs to children, making them addicts.

Today thirteen- or fourteen-year-old children are being given free heroin or cocaine. At the same time, we see babies, who are already addicted to these drugs.

A drug dealer tells children: if you want more drugs, go and sell drugs and bring me the money. Then the child will receive a small amount of drug for its daily habit.

A drug dealer who made a child suffer by making it a heroin or cocaine addict, do you think he can escape from that action, which knowingly and willfully destroyed the mind of a child?

So, when the drug dealer reincarnates, from the very beginning the effect will manifest. The baby's suffering starts already in the intrauterine life, and as soon as the baby is born, it suffers withdrawal symptoms as it does not receive any more drug substance through the mother's blood. The suffering which he created in the past to another child is now taking effect. It is not God who caused this suffering. It is the way cause and effect work.

We can only see the effect, but we cannot see the cause. By analyzing the effect, we can have some conclusion about the cause. You are presently interested in this type of yogic life, with morning and evening meditation, lectures about your astral and your physical body. You learn how to take care of your physical body with āsanas, pranayama and proper diet. To experience all this you must have done some good karma in the past. If not, you would maybe be sitting in a bar or in a restaurant ordering snails, frog legs, fried grasshoppers, chocolate coated ants or birds nest soup.

You must have accrued some yogic knowledge and discipline in the past. This is now acting as a cause. The effect is that you want to get up in the morning and do your *āsana, pranayama,* and hear these yogic lectures.

Ṣaṃsara, the wheel of birth and death

We move from the physical plane to the astral plane. Then again from the astral plane to a physical place. This is called *ṣaṃsara*, the wheel of birth and death. You are rolling through these changes in space and time continuously, from time immemorial. In each life you must get married, have children, go through separation or divorce, experience heartbreaks or a war or another calamity. When you come back in the next life, you will have to repeat the same process. You will have to find again a girl or a boy and get married. Whether you like it or not, whether you are happy or not, you must repeat this continuously.

If life would come only once and we would die at the age of 100, then there would be nothing for us to worry about, as we are all going to die. But we are not satisfied, there is something missing.

Why did you enter this *ṣaṃsara*, this world full of miseries? That is called *karma* or destiny. Time, space and destiny are governed by law. Destiny is not given by someone to you; it does not happen without a cause. *Karma* means both destiny as well as cause and effect.

Sometime in time and space, you had a desire that you want to meditate. Whether this desire occurred ten thousand years ago or more recently, is immaterial. These ten thousand years do not really exist for you. Something happened in the past and the effect is materializing now, and you are all assembling here to meditate.

Soon the sun will be burned out and there will be no more life on planet earth. What will happen then? You will find yourself on another planet, in a different time and space, where you will again assemble to continue from where you left. Everything is cause and effect.

All this is not preplanned, it already exists. Your destiny is like a blueprint which is prepared by you. This house is here now. Before this house came into existence, an architect saw this space. In his mind came a thought how this house should be built. According to these thought forms, he took a pencil and paper and made a blueprint, took the measurements for the house, the hall, the kitchen, the bathrooms, etc. He planned everything on paper. Then the engineer, the carpenters and masons came and built the house exactly according to the measurements of the blueprint.

In the same way you created your destiny first on the thought level. You needed certain things. A desire originated. According to the desire, a blueprint, the seed state formed. These seeds have the power to create your future life.

Karma is stored in the causal or seed body. The seed body contains a version of the innumerable births which you are going to take in the future.

A seed in nature has the capacity to create a huge tree, for example a banyan tree. The banyan tree seed is small, the size of a mustard seed. If you cut it open, you do not see any banyan tree inside, even if you magnify the seed a thousand times. Yet, in the right environment and conditions, this seed has the capacity to create a huge banyan tree. From that tree originate millions of tiny seeds which have the capacity to create an infinite number of trees.

In your seed body lies the capability of creating millions of new bodies so that you may evolve, according to that *karma*. The movement from the seed into the form of a physical body is called evolution, and the movement from a physical body into the seed form is called dissolution. Evolution and dissolution revolve endlessly.

This is how you will reincarnate infinite number of times. All the actions or *karma* which you performed in the past must have a reaction in the form of the powerful force which is hidden in the seed. It can be dormant for thousands of years or it can manifest tomorrow depending upon the environment and the conditions.

Why didn't you come in the 15th century or 14th century, or when Jesus Christ was there or when Moses, Buddha or Lord Kriśna were walking on the planet earth? Which force made you come in this 20th century and will make you die in another 30, 40 or 50 years from now? Latest in 100 years, none of us will be on this planet earth.

This is the power of the karmic seeds which must sprout in time and space according to the conditions of this century. According to the seeds you will live after the death of your physical body in the astral plane for some time, maybe for thousands of years. If you are a good person, you may not even come back during the present iron age. You may only come back in the golden age when everything is peaceful. This is the way *karma* and destiny work.

In this life, you were born in different religions or faiths, with different conditions. You are not lacking any material happiness, you have everything. Yet you came and sit now on a hard floor to hear this yoga philosophy which may be a little boring or foreign to you, or you even do not believe it. And you are chanting all those foreign words that may not have any meaning to you. What force made you come to chant this with full faith? You had this experience in the past and this has brought you here. We are restarting from were we left. So also, what you learn and do today is not gone. It goes into the seeds of the subconscious mind and these seeds will cause you to come to some other place where again you will be chanting and meditating.

If it is your *karma*, you will be discussing with other yogis, svamis and various types of spiritual people until you reach the time and the state where the seed itself is burned. Then it can not sprout anymore, you will be liberated. All desires vanish at that time.

As long as desires exist, you must perform actions, which will have reactions, which in turn will create your destiny with the possibility to create more actions and more seeds.

To get out of this endless cycle of time and space, of karma and destiny, there is only one way: Desires must stop, thoughts must stop. This is what you are doing in meditation. When you will reach a state, where the mind is perfectly still, where there is no more time, no more strife, no more desires, — then you are perfectly satisfied.

In perfect awareness lies perfect satisfaction. There will be no more need to act, there will be no more *karma*, you will be a liberated person.

In this liberated state you realize that you are without old age, without death, without motion. It is called the transcendental state.

The Power of the Last Thought

During the process of dying all important events will appear in front of your mind as well as the most important thoughts which you created during your lifetime. The thoughts of your mental lake will be churned like cream when it is transformed into butter. From that process will arise the last thought of your life. It will be the cream of thought, which will come to the top from both the subconscious and conscious levels of the mind. This last thought determines what you are going to be, what kind of life and which kind of body you are going to have in the future.

Whether you are going to have an animal, a human, an angel or a supra-angel body—all this is determined by your last thought. You may have to take another human body to continue your evolution with parents, relatives, children and grandchildren. All these will be determined by the last thought. Whether you will be a businessman, an engineer, a scientist, a doctor or a yogi will depend on the last thought, which will be the cream of all your thoughts.

During the process of dying, your subconscious mind may be revolving in innumerable thoughts. But none of these thoughts can really take hold of you during these last moments, only the most powerful and specific thought of your life will come up.

There are people who practice 200 *malas* of *japa* (*mantra* repetition) every day throughout their life. At the time of death, the last thought will be the *mantra*. The power of thought will bring up the *mantra*.

After death you will go to one of seven planes. The access to each of these planes depends on the good or bad actions or thoughts which you created, your merits and demerits. Besides these seven higher planes there are also seven lower planes, called the nether lands. In the west you speak about the seventh heaven. What is meant by this? It means that a person is on the highest plane, the seventh plane, were sages and prophets go.

You don't have to worry about the highest planes, because you do not have the kind of credit card which is accepted there. You may have to be happy with the lower planes. The fourth and fifth plane is for very advanced yogis and sages. The first plane is for ordinary people.

Depending on the good and bad karma of your life, after you die, you can only stay in the astral plane for a limited time. According to your karma you will have to leave back into a new incarnation. Advanced karma yogis can go to a very high plane, where their happiness and joy is immense.

Everything is thought, the whole astral plane is nothing but thought. Thought is all that exists there. Everything is created there by your own thoughts, according to your happiness and joy. Heaven is a thought world.

The energy of the last thought corresponds to a particular *chakra* or energy centre. For example, the manipura chakra, the third *chakra*, is only for people who actually have entered the spiritual path and have some spiritual awakening and spiritual experience. So, most of the sincere yoga students can reach the third plane in one life. After death they go to the third plane in their awareness. If you the reach the fourth plane, you are advanced, you are already an adept in yoga. Everything is according to your *akashic* record, the spiritual record which corresponds to the accumulation of all your thoughts. Nothing you have done, good or bad, is lost.

In the Bhagavad Gita, Ārjuna asks Lord Krishna:

VI, 37. "He who is unable to control himself though he has the faith, and whose mind wanders away from Yoga, what end does he meet, having failed to attain perfection in Yoga, O Krishna?"

VI, 38. "Fallen from both, does he not perish like a rent cloud, supportless, O mighty-armed (Krishna), deluded on the path of Brahman?"

Lord Krishna replies:

VI 40. "O Ārjuna, neither in this world, nor in the next world is there destruction for him; none, verily, who does good, O My son, ever comes to grief!"

VI 41. "Having attained to the worlds of the righteous and, having dwelt there for everlasting years, he who fell from Yoga is reborn in the house of the pure and wealthy."

VI 42. "Or he is born in a family of even the wise Yogis; verily a birth like this is very difficult to obtain in this world."

Suppose you went to high school up to the ninth grade, and then you went to the army, maybe you were sent to Vietnam. After your return you want to finish your studies. Will you start at the kindergarten level? No, you will be able to continue your studies from the level at which you left them.

Anything you learnt, any discipline you developed in your life, also your capacity to repeat God's name, is not lost. It is recorded in the *akashic* record. These impressions remain in the subconscious mind. That is why, at the time of death, the stream of thought which will arise, will allow you to continue your evolution in the astral plane. If you cannot be happy here, you are also not going to be happy in the heaven.

Therefore, you must try to change your thought currents as much as you can. It is the same mind which is going to evolve. If you are a business person who is continuously thinking about the stock market, you will be thinking of the same functions also after death. You will not be able to find any peace. That is called hell.

All depends on your mental identification. Imagine you have a son and receive a telegram that he died in the Vietnam war. You will be in an extremely unhappy, powerless and painful state. But actually, your son did not die in Vietnam. The telegram was sent to the wrong person. Your boy is still alive. But this makes no difference, you are still going to suffer. It is not the death of the son which causes the suffering, it is your own identification with that death.

Or imagine that you wake up one morning and receive a telegram that you become a millionaire because you won the lottery. Your mind is now caught in this thought, and you are happy. But then comes another telegram, that you will not be able to get this money until you are 50 years old.

Thought plays the part. Change the patterns of your thoughts if you want to change your life to a life of happiness. What you are now is nothing but your thoughts. Avoid thoughts of another person's defects. The nature of the mind is that it becomes that on which it thinks intensely. Thus, if you think of the defects of another person, your mind will be charged with these vices and defects at least for the time being.

He who knows this psychological law will never indulge in censoring others or in finding fault in the conduct of others. He will see only good and praise others. This practice enables one to progress in concentration and contemplation. Try to face your enemies. Try to face the person you don't like. How hard this is, is it not? But if you learn to do that, what a strong thought this will be, what a thought power will develop at the time? So do not just try seeing every defect.

Even if I know that the other person may have many defects. So what? I may have many defects, too. Where is imperfection? Imperfection is in the body and mind. When the sages say, he is perfect, what is meant by that? Does it mean body and mind are perfect? The sage is identifying with the Soul which is eternally perfect. A sage will not identify with a defective state.

The last thought determines the future birth, the future destiny. Lord Krishna says in the Bhagavad Gita:

VIII,6: "Whosoever at the end leaves the body, thinking of any being, to that being only does he go, O son of Kunti (Arjuna), because of his constant thought of that being!"

VIII,10: "At the time of death, with unshaken mind, endowed with devotion and by the power of Yoga, fixing the whole life-breath in the middle of the two eyebrows, he reaches that resplendent Supreme Person."

Suppose you think of a specific deity, then you will go to that particular plane. Some people think of Śiva, they go to Kailas, others think of Vishnu they go to Vaikunta, others go to Krishna, so there are different astral planes where they will be drawn.

All the seven heavens, even the seventh heaven itself, is eventually dissolved in the cosmic pralaya (unmanifested state), because nothing is eternal. All the galaxies and all the astral planes eventually dissolve.

Even if you go to the sixth or seventh heaven, this is not a permanent place. The lower planes will dissolve quicker; in the higher planes you can stay longer. In the highest plane you meet with the beginning of time or Brahma, so you don't come back. There all beings will wait until another creation takes place and another universe will be created with new planets and galaxies.

If you constantly practice the fixing of the mind on God, then you will automatically think of God even at the time of your departure.

So the worship, the āsanas, the discipline, the pranayama you are doing, all this will enable you to fix your mind at the last moment of your death, because that will be the most powerful thought—you will be able to fix the mind in the way you want.

Ordinary people are torn by the current of prana, the life force which needs to be withdrawn from the 72,000 *nadis* back into the astral body. It is like withdrawing electricity from a grid and can be very painful. To withdraw the prana from the body at will, at the time of death, is difficult. But the advanced yogi has no problem because he knows how to control the prana, and how to direct the prana from the left and right side into the central canal. At the time of death this will happen automatically.

If all your life you meditate on *"Om Namah Śivaya"* or *"OM Namo Narayanaya"*, then naturally this most important part of your mind will come as the last thought. Therefore, we continuously try to keep our thoughts in a positive state.

Karma, Rebirth and Freedom

Your karmic energy is constantly spent. It is like the oil in a lamp which is slowly being spent by the burning wick. When all the oil is depleted, what remains is ash without any trace of oil. If there is oil, the lamp will burn.

Due to *prarabdha*, the effect of the actions of past lives manifesting in the present life, there is *karma* which is allotted to this body. Prana revolves and the body lives. *Karma* is the energy which makes this body move and function.

Your body is like the wick in the oil lamp. Once the *karmic* oil is gone, once the *karma* allotted to this physical body is slowly exhausted, your body cannot function anymore. Then your existence in this physical dimension ends.

I am teaching yoga, because my *karma* prompts me to do this. I am not able to do anything else in this life with this body, because that is not my karmic energy.

As past *karma* materializes or takes it's fruit, then this body reacts to this particular condition. That is why one person is a yoga teacher, a scientist, an engineer, a philosopher, a thief or a bank robber.

It is due to *karmic* tendencies that the body functions in a particular way. Once the *karma* is worked out or exhausted, this body will be thrown back into the food cycle. It came from the food chain, and it must go back to the food chain.

You are not this body. This body is not you. It just came because of *karma*. This *karmic* vehicle is composed of the 5 elements, earth, water, fire, air and ether. These include solid elements like iron, magnesium, as well as up to 70 percent water. All these have come from the food cycle and will go back into the food chain. Anything that is composed, will decompose. The body is composed of this matter and will decompose soon. Earth to earth and ash to ashes.

But that doesn't mean that your life will come to an end. You will continue to exist, just like you also exist during your dreams, at night. After the death of the physical body, you go to the next dimension, according to your *karma*.

Once your *karma* in that dimension is exhausted, you are again reborn in a physical body which is suitable to continue your *karma*. This can be compared to the *karma* of the dream state. Once it is exhausted, you wake up and become again aware of the physical body.

This is called *samsara cakra*, the wheel of birth, death and rebirth. You are born in different countries, and you have different types of professional life. You are tired of this *samsara cakra*.

This is beautifully presented by *Adi Sankaracarya* in *Bhaja Govindam*, verse 21:

punarapi jananam punarapi maraṇam
punarapi jananījaṭhare śayanam,
iha samsāre bahudustāre
kṛpayā'pāre pāhi murāre.
"Being born again, dying again, and again lying in the mother's womb; this *samsara* is extremely difficult to cross over. Save me, O *Kriśna*, through your infinite compassion."

Rebirth is not limited to the womb of a human mother. It includes animal wombs, like a tiger, a cobra, a mosquito or a fly. It is said that we pass through forty thousand wombs before reaching a human womb.

From the human rebirth, there is still a long journey ahead. You can go to an angelic womb or a demoniacal womb, until you find a way to escape from this *saṃsara cakra*.

Therefore you seek a teacher to show you the path to escape from the wheel of birth and death: you must learn to transcend time and space by stilling the mind. That is the secret. As long as the mind fluctuates, this *saṃsara cakra* will continue, and you will be reborn.

You cannot stay even in the angelic body in the heavens. It is like going on a vacation in a hotel. You can enjoy the vacation only as long as long as you can pay for your stay. In the same way, heaven and hell are only temporary places to work out your good *karma* or bad *karma*. They are not permanent places.

There is no eternal damnation or eternal hell. Even an ordinary person who goes to jail for a life sentence, after a certain number years is given parole and is free again. Now there is the choice to change one's habits, or to go back to the same previous negative actions and be punished again.

In the same way, hell is only a temporary situation, where you pay for your negative actions. Then you will be released. There is neither eternal hell nor eternal heaven.

Only when you transcend time, space and causation by stilling the mind through the practice of meditation, you can become free from the cycle of birth and death.

Though you are now born in Spain, France, Germany, Italy, America, or Canada – your past *saṃskaras* or impressions of *yogic* knowledge were accumulated in *Bharatavarśa* or India.

At the same time many souls which are born in India have strong western *saṃskaras*. They drink, eat meat and indulge in the activities which are typical to the western civilizations.

You have already done much *sadhana* or spiritual practices, and you are continuing these practices in this life to reach a higher stage. I try to give you different instructions how to transcend body and mind and how to still the mind; all the techniques which we use here in the ashram are meant to still the mind.

The *āmritabindu ūpanisad*, verse 2, says:

*mana eva manushyanam
karanam bandha-mokshayoh
bandhaya visayasango
muktyai nirvisayam manah*
"For man, mind is the cause of bondage and mind is the cause of liberation. Mind absorbed in sense objects is the cause of bondage, and mind detached from the sense objects is the cause of liberation."

The mind is like a ladder. If you use the ladder properly, it will take you to the height which you want to reach. But a drunken person who tries to climb the ladder, will fall and break his head or even lose his life.

The mind is the ladder which can take you to the highest plane or liberation if you know how to control and train it, the way we learn it here. But an uncontrolled mind, which goes from one pleasure centre to the next, is like a drunken driver; such a mind will take you to hell.

Evolution and Reincarnation

The ultimate aim of *yoga sadhana* (practice) is to step out of *saṃsara*, the cycle of births and deaths. As long as *Śiva* is resting in *sahasrara cakra* and *Śakti* is seated at the end of the spina in the *muladhara cakra*, reincarnation will take place after the physical death.

Śiva and *Śakti* are separated by six stages or *chakras*: *ajna cakra* (forehead), *viśuda cakra* (throat), *anahata cakra* (heart), *manipura cakra* (solar plexus), *svadhisthana cakra* (genitals) and *muladhara cakra* (base of the spine). As long as the energy, the *Śakti* or the *kundalini*, is resting in the *muladhara cakra*, the experience will be gross. We only understand what we see through our eyes, hear through our ears, smell and taste through our physical senses. It seems impossible to consider the existence of anything beyond these faculties.

But the *Śakti* cannot stay in that state forever. As evolution takes place we start thinking "Is the only reality what we see in this world? Is there anything beyond that? There must be another dimension." This is how evolution starts. The *Śakti* starts manifesting, and the upwards process takes place. At that point, money cannot give satisfaction, nor do sensual pleasures. The energy will start vibrating and we start seeking, looking and asking "What to do?" This asking and seeking will lead to a teacher, to a line of teaching. This is called awakening of the *Kundalini Śakti*.

From the *muladhara cakra* (element earth), the *Śakti* moves to the next level, the *svadhisthana cakra* (element water), then to *manipura cakra* (element fire), to *anahata cakra* (element air), to *viśuda cakra* (element ether), to *ajna cakra* (the mind) and from the mind into *Śiva*, in the *sahasrara cakra*. Now you are liberated. Now *Śiva* and *Śakti* are one. You are a realized soul. No more birth, no more death. You are happy. I Am That I Am.

Until you reach this state of liberation you will continue to reincarnate. Suppose you will die having arrived at the second centre; then you will reincarnate from the second plane. There are six planes, the seventh is the transcendental plane or heaven. At a higher step of evolution, one does not go to the first heaven, but to the third or to the fourth or even fifth heaven. Great masters like Jesus, go to the sixth and seventh heaven.

Reincarnation takes place according to the energy level. There are dimensions with a much higher evolution. We have been brought back to this planet earth, a place of low evolution, where the energy is still in a very gross state. That is why we are going to destroy this planet soon, maybe with a nuclear bomb.

If you are highly evolved then you don't have to come back to this planet. By your thought you will be drawn in another direction. There are numerous other planets, other universes. When the energy vibration is very high, we call it heaven. It's not made of soft matter, nor flowers and colors, it is unimaginable for our mind to comprehend. Everything is finer, more beautiful than anything we can see on our gross level.

The purpose of yoga is to make us realize that God did not only create this planet earth with a few human beings, some Jews, a few Arabs, Hindus, men and women, Chinese, Cubans, Russians, a few Americans, etc. This is not the end of creation. There are so many galaxies. Our earth, our solar system, our sun, all these are only one tiny speck. At this very moment several suns are dying, several galaxies are disappearing or appearing. But we think that the planet earth is all that exists.

Different radio and television stations are transmitting. The transmission takes place in the same atmosphere, but the stations do not interfere with one another, because each one has a different wavelength. So also, the parallel universes, or the seven heavens or astral heavens, are not far away from each other. Their vibration or wave lengths are either so high or so low that we are not able to perceive them. Mediums who possess a special gift, like Marilyn Rossner for example, can connect to some of these lower heavens. Beings who are dead will appear as astral energies and communicate. The parallel universes or heavens are not far away, they are all around us. But their wavelength is too high for us to grasp.

Our mind is not blank. We have different experiences from the past, which drew us here today. Our life is similar to a triangle. Point A is birth, then there is upward movement or growth, until the top of the triangle, point B. Here growth stops, and the downward movement follows. Point C is the end, death. After death the line continues and goes back to point A, to a new birth or reincarnation. Again growth, again old age, again death.

You think you have been brought to this earth because of your parents. This is not true. The soul or ātman existed in the past and it will exist infinite times in the future. That soul has no death or birth, it is *Śiva*, God, *Brahman*, the Self. You are here to be reunited with the Self, with *Brahman*.

Experiences of the Astral Body

Within your physical body lies the astral body along with the causal body or seed body, which is still more subtle. For the western mind it is difficult to absorb the idea of another vehicle or body beyond the physical body. The astral body and the causal body always remain together; they never separate until the final emancipation. The understanding of the astral body requires a look at reincarnation and the law of karma.

There is much confusion in the western mind about life here and life hereafter. I am going to ask you some questions. Please try to use pure reasoning, leaving preconceived notions aside, especially any notion of an emotional nature.

Are you sure that you will die one day? Yes, we see that no one here has a doubt about that.

When you die, will you leave your physical body on this earth? Your answer is "yes".

Did Christ take his physical body with him when he went to heaven? You see, this question brings up some emotions and different opinions!

Did Christ breathe and eat when he was alive? — Yes. That means he had a stomach, liver, kidneys, and he also had to go to the bathroom. He had to sleep also. Whether virgin conception or otherwise, Jesus was born from a physical mother, Mother Mary. Baby Jesus was breathing and eating, just like our body. If the infant baby Jesus did not eat, the baby would have died. Would that baby's body have gone to heaven or back into the earth?

Here is the difficulty for the Western mind, because it is written that the disciples of Jesus saw his body appear to them after he had died. But what did they see, was it a physical body or something else? The law of the physical body is that 'what came from earth must go back to earth.'

I eat tomatoes and my body grows like a tomato. After I die, you will bury my body. Suppose you put a tomato plant over me, what happens to the tomato plant? The tomato plant will say 'some time back you ate me, now I am going to eat you.' Many tomatoes grow on the tomb. If you eat these tomatoes, you are actually eating Svami Vishnu.

It is clear that this body came from the food chain. It has not come from anywhere else. Jesus ate food, the food was converted into the body, and this must go back into the food chain.

But there is another vehicle inside the physical body which the soul uses after the physical body goes back to the earth. This astral body is just like the physical body. At the time of physical death, it rises from the physical body. It is the exact replica of what you see now. This is what the disciples of Jesus saw. Because you do not have an idea about the astral body, you cannot explain this event and there is confusion about it.

Suppose it was the physical body which goes up, where can it go? The physical body can exist only in a physical environment. But heaven is not made of physical matter, it is a place of subtle frequencies. These waves are very high. No physical matter can survive there.

As a comparison, bombard the tissues of the physical body with invisible x-rays for a long time, the tissues will be destroyed. When the dentist takes the x-ray of your teeth, he covers the rest of your body with a lead blanket. And even then, it is too dangerous for pregnant women, as the x-rays affect the unborn baby.

The heavenly waves are not made up of matter but of high waves. Your physical body, the earthly matter cannot survive in that system. So, leaving preconceived notions aside, you can understand that the vision of Jesus after the crucifixion was not a manifestation of his physical body. Jesus had the power to move his astral body to a wavelength which his disciples could see.

This happened to me in Canada. I saw Gurudev Sivananda after his physical death, even though Gurudev Sivananda left his physical body in Rishikesh, in the Himalayas, in India. I was in the Laurentian Mountains in Canada, and there I saw Swami Sivananda in my tent. Let me tell you how it happened. Whether you believe it or not, is up to you.

I started the first yoga camp in Val Morin in the Laurentian Mountains in Canada. This kind of yoga vacation and yoga camp happened for the first time in the history of the West. During this yoga summer camp in 1963, I had only 3 staff with me. In the beginning of July, I received a telegram from Rishikesh, that my Master is seriously ill. Naturally I wanted to rush to India to be with my Master during the last moments of his earthly life. I wanted to be near him.

But people had registered for the yoga vacation camp. What was my duty? I could not leave them with the staff, who didn't really know what yoga was. In those days, I did not have any trained yoga teachers with me. Suppose I had asked your advice what would you have said? Stay! Is it not? So, I sent a telegram back asking if it is really serious. Could I wait for a few more days to go? The reply came, that the Master was feeling well again. I was relieved and stayed.

But after three days, the Master's state became worse and he left his physical body in the ashram in Rishikesh in the Himalayas on July 14, 1963. In those days I used to sleep in a tent. The few rooms were given to the guests. One of the staff, called André, also slept in a tent, next to mine. It was the night of July 17. I had received the news that the Master had left. I am not afraid of death. Death has no meaning to me. But I couldn't be there to see him in his last moments. I could not speak to him anymore. I missed the opportunity to see him one last time on this earth. With this terrible mental pain, I went to sleep.

At 4am, while I was still asleep, there was a voice: " Vishnu Swamiji wake up, Vishnu Swamiji wake up." No one used to call me " Vishnu Swamiji" except my Master. I did not get out of bed because it was quite cold in the early morning. I thought maybe André was calling from his tent. Without getting out of my sleeping bag, I shouted from my tent to his tent "André, did you call me?" After some time he answered: "No Swamiji, I didn't call you." I thought that maybe I had heard the voice in my dream. I went to sleep again. Again, the voice came 'Vishnu Swamiji, wake up!' That was not in my dream. I sat up and there was my Master, giving me a message: " Vishnu Swami I am always with you!" I cannot describe that experience.

For a Master, astral travel is easy, it does not take any time, nor do they need any material things for that. They can take atoms from the atmosphere and temporarily make their astral body visible as a physical appearance for us, until these wavelengths disintegrate again.

I was so shocked, I couldn't think of anything. The Master was trying to lift me up to higher planes. I immediately called, "André, get up, you can see the Master." He got up, but he saw only a bright light over my tent. It lasted only for a few minutes. That's the only time I saw the Master in this kind of astral projection after his departure. Many disciples have had the experience of this kind of appearance of their Master.

Now, let us go to another level of understanding: Even ordinary people sometimes see their dead relatives. Especially when there is intense love and attachment. There is the example of an American soldier who died in Vietnam. He died at about 2:00 AM Vietnam time. The time difference between the East coast of America and Vietnam is 12 hours. While her son was at the time in Vietnam, the mother saw her son in her living room at 2 PM East Coast time, and he said "Mother, I am saying goodbye, I won't see you again." She did not believe in astral bodies etc, it was not part of her understanding. She called her husband, 'Honey, I just saw our son here. He said goodbye! I do not understand.' She noted the time. The next day she received a telegram, informing her that her son had died exactly at that time. This is not a unique occurrence, there are several such cases.

The astral body is not composed of matter, and it is not affected by time and space like the physical body. When you are dreaming, you can dream that you are in London or in India. Though you are here, you still feel that you are in India or in London or Paris. So, time and space have no effect in your dream. Your astral body can move at lightening velocity to any dimension it wants.

Here is a more scientific example: A patient is brought for heart surgery and receives anesthesia, so that no pain will be felt. During general anaesthesia, the patient cannot see anything, nor hear what the doctors say. There is also no sense of touch, smell or taste. But the patient is breathing, and the heart is beating. So, the doctors start operating on the heart for 2-3 hours. What happens to the real person during that time?

The real person is in the astral body, moves up to the roof, the ceiling, and from there he is watching the physical body lying on the table. The surgery is successful, the general anesthesia is over, and the patient opens the eyes. After some time, he speaks to the doctor about the whole operation as if he had physically seen it. The doctor replies that this is not possible as he was unconscious. But the patient gives a full description of what the doctor did, the conversation between the nurses and the doctors and what type of instruments were used. He describes in detail the instruments of surgery which he has never seen in his life and how they were used to operate on his heart.

The seeing did not come from the physical eyes, it came from the astral body. The capacity of seeing is actually in your astral body. The physical eyes of the physical body connot see by themselves. It is because the astral body exists in the physical body, that your physical eyes can see.

Another example: A patient just died in an accident, by drowning or from a heart attack. He is brought to the hospital where the doctors try to resuscitate him. When the patient comes back from this state of clinical death, he gives a full description of what the doctors did to revive him. The patient says that he is very unhappy that the doctors resuscitated him, which means that they brought the astral body back into the physical body. The person, while he was clinically dead, tried to communicate to the doctors to tell them: "Don't do anything to me, I am okay here." But the doctors could not hear.

These things are not revealed by yogis; this information is collected by medical doctors such as Dr Raymond Moody in his book "Life after Life". He interviewed many patients who were resuscitated and spoke about the near-death experience.

All these examples, from modern science to traditional thinking, from the example of Jesus, and my own experience, all these can help you to understand the astral existence.

When you practice meditation, *pranayama* and even *āsanas*, and also when an acupuncture doctor uses needles for treatment on the physical body, — all these affect your astral body. The *nadis* and *cakras* are not in the physical body. If you cut open the body, you won't find the *cakras* there. You may find physical nerves, but these are not the astral chakras or astral nerves. They are only physical counterparts. When the physical body dies, the astral body with prana, chakras and nadis departs, none of these remain in the physical body.

Whatever you see in your dream is just a thought. But it could also be astral travel. At that time, the astral body departs from your physical body and remains connected through an astral chord, like an umbilical cord connecting the baby and the mother. The *prana* flows from the astral body to the physical body through that astral chord. Under general anesthesia, the astral body is separated from the physical body, but the chord is still intact. Once this chord is cut off, permanent separation of the astral body and the physical body will happen and the physical body dies.

Sometimes during meditation or even during sleep, people have an astral travel experience, where they are separated from the body. They are very frightened as it is a death-like experience. But there is nothing to worry about. You will come back, as long as the astral chord is intact. The astral chord is only cut if the *karma* for physical death has come. This can also happen in a situation of extreme shock, either from fear or even from extreme happiness.

Lower astral entities

Murders take place every day. A few days ago, a man went into a bar in New York City. There he beat another customer and therefore was not allowed to come back to that bar. The man came back and shot a policeman and several customers inside the bar. Then he shot himself.

Big cities are filled with lower astral entities, because people are killed daily. After being shot or stabbed, they don't know how to get out of this lower astral state. In all major cities there are plenty of ghosts or spirits.

Drinking and gambling places are the areas where these people used to visit when they were alive in their physical body. Suddenly their physical body is thrown off, and what do they do? They just go and sit in the same places, in the same area.

A man rented an apartment in New York in a very fashionable place on 5th Avenue. At night he heard some sounds. He saw a man in his living room, who then went through the window and jumped down to the street. He really thought the man had jumped from the window. He ran down and asked if anyone had seen someone jump from his apartment. No one had seen anything. But he was told that the previous tenant of the flat had committed suicide by jumping from the window. Now this man is reenacting his suicide every night, as he is caught on the lower astral plane, the earthbound state.

During World War II, many millions of people died through bullets and explosions. Their bodies suddenly were torn apart. They became earthbound spirits and many still do not know how to get out of this state. Do not think that soldiers who die in a war just go to heaven.

Peace is not only an urgent need for the people living on this earth. Please understand that many of the people who die a violent death are now mentally disturbed in a completely earthbound state. They need help to adjust and accommodate in the environment of the astral plane from where they will finally move on to their next birth.

Please send your positive thoughts to these people.

Suicide

Sometimes when things get extremely unbearable, then a person may want to get away from this world itself. The person commits suicide, thinking that this would be an escape. Yet this will not help the person in any way. It is like jumping from a hot pan into a burning fire. By suicide the physical body dies, but the painful emotions are all still intact. This prevents the mind from going up into the next plane. People who commit suicide, become earthbound spirits for some time. They cannot get released into the astral world which is what normally happens at the time of death. *(Swami Vishnudevananda)*

Why is suicide considered a sin?

Pleasure and pain in life are respectively the rewards of the good and the bad actions of an individual. If a man suffers, it is a reminder to him to ennoble his life and make his future happy through the performance of good deeds, self-discipline and right effort.

When a person, convicted to a term of imprisonment by the court of law for having committed an offence, escapes from the prison, the law demands that he should be rearrested and given added punishment, because he had not only committed an offence but tried to avoid the punishment therefor. So is the case with trying to escape from one's suffering by inflicting death on oneself, rather than attempting, through self-effort, to improve one's future or accepting philosophically what is beyond all help.

One has, besides, no right to take a life, even though it may be his own, since it is a crime not only in the eyes of God but also in the eyes of social law. The person who commits suicide will suffer more in a spirit-body for some time, and then take a lower form of birth, to work out his *karma*. So, one will not be benefited in any way by committing suicide. *(Swami Sivananda)*

Averting a Suicide

I will give you one more instance, just to illustrate His approach to life. It must be about forty years ago. I was a young doctor in Lucknow. In those days there were no telephones in Rishikesh. I received a letter from Swami Sivananda: "I am sending a patient for you with somebody. Kindly keep the patient, make her all right." That was all. I could not make out, what was wrong with the patient. The "patient" came, she was a young girl, a college student somewhere. She had gone astray and became pregnant. And in those days, this was not easily accepted neither in society nor at home. She had come to the Ganga to commit suicide. A policeman saw her and brought her to the ashram hospital, to obtain help from a doctor. They brought her to Swami Sivananda. The whole ashram was up at once: "How can we keep such a woman? She is a condemned woman! How can we keep such a person in an ashram, just imagine!" Swami Sivananda did not bother. He said: "Keep her" and first sent the letter to me and then the girl. Nobody knew where she was from, nobody knew anything about her. She was a nice, well-educated person and seemed to come from a good family. I was then living with my parents, and they also had old-fashioned ideas. My mother put a big stop and said: "You can't keep this girl in our house. Swami Sivananda is a *sannyasin* (monk), he doesn't know the world. I will not keep her in my house." I was in a terrible situation. Swami Sivananda has sent a patient, and I didn't know where to keep her. She was about seven months pregnant. Where could I keep her for three months? I was in a mess, and the swami who had brought her, went away. I admitted her to the hospital under a lie that she was not well with severe anaemia and all that. For three months I kept her in the hospital and then she delivered a girl. Swami Sivananda had given me the instruction that He should be informed as soon as she delivered. I wired to Him that she had given birth to a girl. You won't believe it, but after ten days a man came to collect her. She was brought to the ashram with the child. You can imagine, who but Swami Sivananda would do such a thing? Even parents will not do this much. Then, among Swami Sivananda's disciples there was a couple who had no children. They were in Andhra Pradesh. Swami Sivananda sent someone, brought them here, and in front of the Master's *Kutir*, on the Ganges bank, a *havan* (fire ceremony) was preformed and the baby was handed over to the couple for adoption. Swami Sivananda told the girl: "Look here my dear girl, you are free now, you can go wherever you want. Go back to your college." And she went back. Can you believe it? Her parents didn't know, her college didn't know. Everyone in the college thought she had gone home and everyone at home thought she was in college. All this happened with the intervention of a saint, Swami Sivananda. No other saint would have done it. I can tell, because I know the reactions in our ashram. In fact, the news spread outside, and other ashram started talking about it. But do you think Swami Sivananda bothered? "Let them talk", he said, "for how long can somebody talk bad about you? After some time they will keep quiet." Nothing bothered Him.

I have told these instances just to show you, how He was, what a supreme love He had for humanity. He never condemned anybody because he went astray. He never condemned anybody because he did something wrong. To him these were all little mistakes, as He said, in His overpowering love. And this overpowering love brought them back. And sometimes when He tried to transform people—of course some of them have been transformed—but others... after exploiting all the love and care, they used to run away. And that of course annoyed people like us. We couldn't understand it; so much love had been given to them. You know what Swami Sivananda used to say? He said: "Let them go. At least the seed is sown. In some life it will sprout. If not in this life, after some lives it will sprout. Nobody can be condemned for life." That was His supreme optimism. That is what He taught us. That should be our ideal. Our ideal should always be beyond our reach. Nobody is bad, nobody is condemnable, and people who make mistakes are bound to improve. That is what we must learn if we want to follow Swami Sivananda. He was like a shepherd. It says in the bible "The Lord is my shepherd and I shall not want." The shepherd, when a sheep goes astray, will go out of his way to bring it back to the flock. That is what He did with us. Whatever we did, whenever we did anything wrong, he didn't mind. He was always kind, He was always loving. He brought us back, and in fact, the more mistakes we made, the more love we got from Him! *(Dr. Devaki Kutty)*

Spiritual Counseling

Srimathi M. had written a pathetic letter, recounting the misfortunes that have visited her, her desperate condition and the causes that often tempt her to commit suicide. By the next post came Swami Sivananda's reply which after entreating her to think, reflect, and face the trials of life with calm endurance, warned her against hasty surrender to emotion.

"Do not commit any such unwise act—you will gain nothing. This will lead to misery and suffering. Life is most precious. It is very difficult to get a human birth. Yield not to emotions. Be bold. Be cheerful. You can attain divinity in this birth and free yourself from birth and death through japa and meditation. May God bless you."
(Svami Venkatesananda)

Question and Answers on Karma

With Swami Sivananda

Question: Why does not the benevolent, kind and all-merciful God help the righteous man and give him happiness? Why does He leave him to the mercies of his *prarabdha karma*?

Swami Sivananda: *Karma* is likened to the wheel. It must be worked out; because the force that set it in motion must be spent. It is a cycle of action and reaction. Just as the arrow once discharged from the bow cannot be withdrawn, even if the hunter feels that he has aimed at a wrong target, *prarabdha karma*, the fruit of those *karmas* performed in previous births that have come up for experience in this present birth, cannot be annulled.

How then does God help His devotee? The all-merciful God does help his devotee by strengthening his will-power, his power of endurance to bear the fruits of *karma* with a cheerful countenance. The devotee is certainly not left to the mercy of his *prarabdha karma;* he is beautifully clothed in the protective shield of His grace. Just as in the worst winter and violent storm, you remain unaffected in your own house and in your warm clothing, the devotee (though to the onlookers he is poor, sick or suffering) does not feel that he is suffering at all and is ever happy and blissful in His remembrance.

Question: A man doing a wrong thing argues that he is doing it because of his *karma*; and he does not even try not to do it, because it gives him immediate happiness. How to impress upon him not to do it?

Swami Sivananda: *Karma* does not compel a man to do wrong actions. *Saṃskaras* (habitual mental impressions) do, to a certain extent. But God has bestowed free will on man, with which to make or mar his career. Man has no *bhoga-svatantrata* or the freedom to enjoy or suffer as that factor is governed by *karma*. But, he has got *karma-svatantrata* or freedom to do good or evil. He can substitute good *saṃskaras* in place of the old vicious *saṃskaras* by the power of reflection, willpower and continued practice of good actions.

That evil seems to give immediate happiness is the greatest temptation and the greatest obstacle to the cultivation of virtues; and it can be removed only by discrimination and experience. Contemplation over the ultimate and permanent damage done to the very soul of man by the evil actions, and the harm he is causing to the entire society itself by his evil, ought to compel a man to desist from evil action however pleasant it might appear superficially. There is no short-cut to this really serious problem; the wicked heart will not yield easily. And therefore, our ancients have exalted *satsang*. Constant association with the wise and spiritually evolved persons alone can remove these wrong notions from the mind of the wicked one.

Question: Is it possible for a soul with a male body to take a female body in the next incarnation?

Swami Sivananda: O, yes. The soul must undergo various experiences in different bodies. In the male body, the soul experiences the qualities of boldness, strength, etc., and patience, mercy, kindness, forgiveness, etc. in the female body. Moreover, neither a man is a full man nor a woman a full woman. There is woman in man and man in woman also. There are animal traits also in man. There is the dog in some men, there is the donkey in some, there is the jackal in some and the tiger in others. Depending on which quality is predominant, the soul takes a body with that particular quality in the next incarnation. Therefore, develop divine qualities. You will evolve quickly and become divinity itself in the end.

Question: What is your conclusive opinion about rebirth? Do you really believe that there is rebirth?

Swami Sivananda: Yes, undoubtedly there is rebirth.

First, you have several miraculous instances of young boys and girls suddenly exhibiting great knowledge. A young girl, who has never studied any book, recites the *Gita*. How do you account for it except by the fact that she had mastered the *Gita* in her previous birth, and that by the grace of the Lord, that knowledge has come to the conscious part of her mind in this birth too?

Further, rebirth is a necessity for the soul's evolution. Perfection cannot be achieved in one birth. Even to develop some cardinal virtues it might take several births. If you wish to attain Self-realization, you have to achieve perfection in all the virtues. You have to achieve perfect self-purification. So, rebirth is a necessity for the *jiva's* (individual soul) evolution.

Have you seen the caterpillar moving from one leaf to another? It will reach the edge of one leaf; then project itself; it will catch hold of another leaf, and then only will it entirely leave the first leaf. The *jiva*, too, goes about like this. Even before it leaves one body, it has made another (gross or subtle) body according to its *karmas* and desires; and it enters this new body with all the *samskaras* (habitual mental impressions) and *vasanas* (subtle desires).

Question: What is the interval between death and the next birth? Where does the soul dwell during the period between death and rebirth?

Swami Sivananda: The interval between death and rebirth varies from person to person. It may be two years, or it may be two hundred years, or more. There is no hard and fast rule. If the attachment to the world is very intense, a *jiva* (individual soul) may be born again immediately after death. There is a girl in Dehra Dun who remembers her past life. She took her present birth four years after she died in her previous life. Those who have done a lot of virtuous actions remain in heaven for a long time, for two hundred or three hundred years, before the are reborn on earth.

A wicked man will go to another region. You may call it hell. Or it may be a place where he may not get the objects of enjoyment that he wants. A man addicted to drinking may not get liquor there. It may be a place like a jail where one has to break the stones and do such other hard work. But if one has done virtuous deeds, if one is a philanthropist, who has dug public wells, built charitable hospitals, etc., he will go to heaven where he will enjoy for a long time.

Question: I would like to know very much where my husband's soul is at present. I shall be obliged if you could explain to me what happens to the soul after death and what merits we could do for the peace of the departed soul and whether he could see or hear us mortals. Is there any truth in what the spiritualists say that we could commune with the dead through a thing called 'medium' and is it really the dead person who answers?

Swami Sivananda: Do not allow yourself to be fascinated by spiritualism, mediumship, crystal gazing, etc. They will lead you astray. Communication with the dead and talking with the dead are all fads which have no connection with real spirituality. The purpose of life is different. The goal is to realize the essential imperishability of your Self. This alone will confer perfect bliss and peace.

The spirit is neither born nor does it die. Like a person passing from one room to another, the soul passes from one plane of existence to another. In the period between death and rebirth, the individual works out a certain portion of his *karmas* in subtler spheres. At the appointed time, the soul takes up a new body again.

The best means of ensuring peace for the departed is to do *kirtan* (*mantra* chanting), increase your *japa* (*mantra* repetition), relieve other people's distress by selfless service and charity, and do earnest prayer.

Do not try to commune with the departed soul of your husband. Communion with the departed soul will stand in the way of its onward march to higher blissful regions and make it earth-bound. Do not try to drag your husband down. It will disturb his peace. The spirit-guide which controls the medium is ignorant and deceitful. It utters falsehood.

Question: Can a person really help others in this world, or is it that such an idea is due to a delusion in the mind? Is it not true that a man can rise or fall only as a result of his own *karma* and that the *karmas* of others can have no effect on him? Are not the circumstances that a person meets with earned by his own actions? Can a person take initiative and change the circumstances of himself as well as of others?

Swami Sivananda: Surely one can take the initiative. He can do good to himself and to others. He can determine the circumstances and environments. Just see how much one can do for others, how much one can really assist them in the relative plane. One can impart knowledge to the illiterate and the ignorant, extend monetary help to the poor and the needy.

One can educate the orphans and contribute to the institutions that take care of the children. Indeed, one can spend not only his entire earnings, but something more! Why should there be any doubt in regard to one's being really helpful to others? Take the example of Gandhiji. Did he not do immense service and good to the nation and to the world at large?

Question: How to free ourselves from *karma*, Swamiji?

Swami Sivananda: Feel, as you do your daily duties, that you are only a witness of all that goes on around you, of even your own actions. This is called *sakśi bhav*. You should inwardly realize that you are different from the active principle in you. This is the method of *Vedanta*.

There is the other, easier, but equally potent method of *nimitta bhav*. Feel that the Lord alone is the real doer of all actions and that you are an instrument in His hands. Your actions will be transformed into worship of the Lord, and you will not be bound to them. Work without expectation of any reward and without egoism. Root out the idea of agency; feel, "I am not the doer". You will be freed from the shackles of *karma*. You will not accumulate new *karma*. Allow your *prarabdha karma* to work out; and you will attain liberation.

Question: Why is suicide considered a sin?

Swami Sivananda: Pleasure and pain in life are respectively the rewards of the good and the bad actions of an individual. If a man suffers, it is a reminder to him to ennoble his life and make his future happy through the performance of good deeds, self-discipline and right effort.

When a person, convicted to a term of imprisonment by the court of law for having committed an offence, escapes from the prison, the law demands that he should be rearrested and given added punishment, because he had not only committed an offence but tried to avoid the punishment therefor. So is the case with trying to escape from one's suffering by inflicting death on oneself, rather than attempting through self-effort to improve one's future or accepting philosophically what is beyond all help.

One has, besides, no right to take a life, even though it may be his own, since it is a crime not only in the eyes of God but also in the eyes of social law. The person who commits suicide will suffer more in a spirit-body for a period of time, and then take a lower form of birth, to work out his Karma. So, one will not be benefited in any way by committing suicide.

Question: The *ātman* is different from the body and is not affected by the latter's doings. The body is reborn a number of times according to its Karma and goes through life and death as per the Supreme Will. If this is so, then who goes to hell or heaven?

Swami Sivananda: The real experiencer of anything, in an individualistic way, is neither the Self nor the physical body. It is the mind that is the centre of individuality, that individualizes and imprisons a ray of the *ātman* in what is called the individual soul. And it is this mind, as embodied in the subtle body, that undergoes the pleasure of heaven or the pains of hell, or for that matter, any experience through a gross or a subtle body.

The mind appears to have consciousness on account of there being a ray of the *ātman* in it, in the form of a reflection, very much limited by its own constitution. Hence it will be clear that the individuality of a person is as much real or unreal as a reflection of a real object.

Though everything happens according to the Supreme Will, the *karma* of the individual determines the form or shape of the experience that is to be had under the dispensation of this Will. It is not the *ātman* or the body that has any type of relative experience, though the body is a gross means of experience; it is the mind that has all this.

Question: We see a very good man suffering too much. Why? The answer may be: "Because of his previous *karma* in his previous birth". This we can trace back to the day of creation.

Swami Sivananda: The law of *karma* is inexorable. Every one reaps the fruits of his previous births. A good man only will suffer a lot, because he is hurrying up in the spiritual march. Many of his evil *karmas* have to be worked out and purged out quickly to hasten his salvation in this very birth. But, God gives him extraordinary power of endurance through His grace. An aspirant or a good man gets many difficulties and sufferings. But he rejoices even in sufferings and destitution on account of the descent of the Lord's grace. He voluntarily welcomes these sufferings. The only best thing in this world is pain or suffering, because it is the eye-opener towards God.

Question: Does the soul take a new body in one year? Does it take ten years? How long does one live upon the subtler planes before reappearing on the earth plane?

Swami Sivananda: There is no definite period of time in this matter. In main, two factors decide this issue, viz., the nature of the individual *karma* and the last impression before death. It may vary from hundreds of years to a few months even. Those that work out some of their *karmas* in other planes in subtler regions take a considerable time before entering a fresh body. The interval is very long, for a year of the earth period passes off as a single day on the celestial plane. There is an instance cited where, seeing the amazement and admiration of foreign tourists at the imposing ruins of certain ancient monuments, a saint present in the vicinity remarked that some of those people had fashioned those monuments centuries ago.

A very sensual individual with strong craving or one with intense attachment sometimes is reborn quickly. Also in cases where life is cut short by a violent death or a sudden unexpected accident, the *jiva* resumes the thread very soon. Usually, in such cases of immediate rebirth, the *jiva* often remembers many of the events of its previous life. It recognizes its former relatives and friends and identifies its old home and familiar objects. This sometimes leads to very queer developments. There are some instances where a murdered person, being reborn, has declared the manner of his death and revealed the identity of the killer in the recent past.

But such cases of immediate rebirth are not common. Generally, for an average individual, the interval between death and rebirth happens to be a considerable period measured in terms of earth time. Persons who have done much good *karma* spend a great deal of time on the *daivic* plane before being born again. Great souls, spiritually advanced persons, wait for a long time before reincarnating.

Question: I never intend to do any evil action. Is it my responsibility when I do it? If it is, will God forgive me? If He forgives me, what about the fruit of that action? I write to you candidly, for I have chosen you to be my noble guide. Please forgive me and help me.

Swami Sivananda: You are certainly responsible for the action. God never forgives. Action brings on its own fruits. Through *prayascitta* or expiatory rites you can destroy the evil effects of a bad action. You actually suffer in *prayascitta*. Hence the evil effects are washed off. The evil *karma* will not follow you to the next birth. Sincere repentance, *japa*, fasting and charity can destroy the evil effects of bad *karma*. In repentance you actually suffer. This serves to wash off the evil effects of the bad action. Repentance must be done with a contrite heart. You must not repeat the evil action again.

Question: How is it that we see many wicked persons flourishing in this world while the good souls suffer? Why is God merciful to some and heartless to others?

Swami Sivananda: This is an age-old question, as old as the world itself. The great *Bhiṣma* shed tears when he was on his death-bed. When questioned why he cried, he replied that the *pandavas* were great devotees of the Lord and always abided by the laws of *dharma*. Above all, the Lord was constantly with them in the form of *Kriṣna*. And yet they underwent so much suffering.

Some wicked persons do flourish in this world of hypocrisy, but it does not mean that they are free from suffering. The really good souls do not suffer as much as the 'flourishing' wicked ones, for peace is in the hearts of the former. To be able to abide by the ideals they hold sacred is by itself a great cause of happiness. The welfare and the misery of people can be explained only in terms of the law of *karma*.

Good persons suffer because of the mistakes they had committed in their past incarnations. Wicked persons, who seem to be well off, are now reaping the results of their past good actions, but will have to pay the price of their present ones, later. It is the law of *karma* that lifts God above all the good and the bad conditions of man. If God were made responsible for the material state of affairs of the individual or the enjoyment or suffering of man, then God would cease to be God, for a partial God, dishing out favours to some and withholding them from the others, would be no God at all.

With Swami Vishnudevananda

Question: Is it possible to avoid *karma*?

Swami Vishnudevananda: If my present life would have come to an end today, I would not be sitting here today with you sharing this lecture. It shows that my *karma* on the earth and the people I am supposed to meet is not over. Living or dying is not really the issue, the important question is whether my *karma* is completed.

Question: Can good *karma* balance out bad *karma*?

Swami Vishnudevananda: If you are going to do more good *karma* your accumulated *karma* will be more, good credit is there.

If I borrow one thousand dollars from you, then I owe you, is it not? On the other hand I gave a hundred thousand dollars in charity. Now you come and request me to return the money which I owe you. Can I just say that there is no need to give the one thousand dollars to you, because I donated so much in charity? I still owe you.

Similarly, if you have done one small bad *karma* and a hundred good karmas, you will enjoy the hundred good *karmas* but you will also have to work out the one bad *karma*.

Question: Is it possible to reduce the forces of bad *karma* by spiritual practices and meditation?

Swami Vishnudevananda: Only once you reach God realization, Self realization, at that moment all the accumulated *karma* will be destroyed. Imagine there is a storehouse full of seeds waiting to be planted in the spring. If you dry-roast all the seeds, they will not germinate, even if you plant them at the perfect time and under the best conditions.

There will be no more future births for you. What remains is the *prarabdha karma* or the fruits of past good or bad actions which are attached to this body, to this birth. However for the God realized person there is no more identification neither with good nor with bad *karma*.

Question: What is the connection between lifespan and *karma*?

Swami Vishnudevananda: For this life, *prarabdha karma* has already been allotted, and this includes the time when you will reach the end of your life. Once the *karma* is exhausted, the time for your body on this planet is over. The body comes from the food chain, or pizza, ice cream and bananas. And many creatures like germs and worms are waiting to eat your dead body. It can be compared to a leased car. As long as you pay your dues, you can keep the car. But the moment you stop payment, your car will be taken away. Similarly, you don't own this physical body, the *annamaya kośa*, it has been leased to you for a short time from the animal kingdom or vegetable kingdom. It has to complete the cycle by going back into the food chain. As soon as the *prarabdha karma* is over, this *annamaya kośa* will disintegrate. In the future life, you will receive another *annamaya kośa* or physical body.

Question: Is there always responsibility for our actions?

Swami Vishnudevananda: An action can touch you only if you can understand and take the responsibilities of an action. A child or a madman cannot perform any sensible action.

Question: Is it possible to stop all *karma*?

Swami Vishnudevananda: Once you have experienced the effect of any *prarabdha*, whether it is a good or a bad *karma*, that *karma* is finished. While we are working out *prarabdha karma* we are simultaneously creating new *karma* which will go into the *karma* bank.

Whichever *karma* you are undergoing, you can still attain God realization through your self-effort. But even a self realized soul will undergo *prarabdha karma*. He or she may be starving one day.

Question: Can *karma* influence my present self-effort?

Swami Vishnudevananda: Your present self-effort will be modified both by your past *karma* and by your *ṣamskaras* or habitual tendencies.

Due to your past *karma*, you came to this Yoga Teachers' Training Course. Whether you are going to finish this course or whether you will run away in the middle, will depend on your *ṣamskaras* (tendencies). In the atmosphere of the ashram and with the support by a teacher you will be able to counteract old *ṣamskaras* and change your future through self-effort. For some, this ashram appears to be like hell. They feel like a fish out of water and cannot wait to finish this course and leave this place. Others are enjoying their stay so much that they do not want to leave from here.

It depends on the *samskaras*. Many make the effort and stay even if it is painful. Definitely your *karma* will modify your action.

Question: "Do sages have *karma*?"

Swami Vishnudevananda: What you are experiencing at present is nothing but the results of the efforts which you have made in the past. Therefore, you need to experience the fruit of this *karma* in this life. If you don't want to accept your *karma*, nature will force you anyway. Then you will cry and be unhappy. Therefore, we should accept our *karma* and be happy like the sages. Even sages, saints and yogis undergo different *prarabdha karmas*. No one is free from it. Do not try to change these *karmic* patterns. Even sages will not do this. Only sometimes they can change a *prarabdha karma* for a specific reason and only for a short time. But they will suffer even more afterwards.

Swami Sivananda held a Parliament of Religions in his ashram in Rishikesh in April 1953. Delegates came from all over India, to represent all religions. But then, the Master developed severe lumbar pain. He could not move from the bed during the days before the Parliament and was completely bedridden. The doctor said it would be difficult for him to walk or to even get up from the bed. The Master's house was right on the banks of the Ganga River, and he would have to walk up the steep foot path up the hill to the Conference Hall where all the functions would be taking place. To our amazement, about an hour before the conference began, Swami Sivananda simply got out of bed and started to walk and reached the conference hall well before the activities began. He sat for two to three hours, inaugurated the conference, and gave the opening address. Afterwards he walked down, went back to bed, and could not move again. The Master did that only once, not for his body's sake but for the conference.

There was another yogi who was invited by a Maharaja to stay in a special cottage in the royal garden surrounded by beautiful flowers, with attendants to take care of anything he would need. Every evening the great guru came and addressed the royal family about yoga, meditation and philosophy. The king was very much devoted to the guru and the guru was fond of the king. After the satsang, the guru would go back to his cottage and the king would go to his palace.

One night, the attendants heard a noise coming from the guru's room. When they looked through the window, they saw great guru rolling on the floor with stomach pain, making horrible noises, kicking his feet, and knocking the head against the floor. The attendants could not understand how a great master could have such a stomachache. They reported what they had seen to the king. The following night the king himself came to the door of the cottage and announced "the king is here to see you". There was no answer, only the painful sound from the guru's voice due to the stomachache. At last, the guru opened the door and asked the king to come inside. The guru appeared to be quite normal and peaceful, as if nothing had happened.

Only some noise was coming through the locked door of the meditation room. The king asked who was in the room. The guru replied that no one was there. When the meditation room door was opened, the deer skin on which the guru used to meditate, was jumping up and down with pain. The king asked why this was happening. The guru replied that there was nothing wrong with the deer skin: "I was having a terrible stomachache. Then you came and interrupted the pain. So, I temporarily passed on the pain to the deer skin. When you go back to the palace, I will take the pain back from the deer skin.

Question: What is first: free will or *karma*?

Swami Vishnudevananda: In a circle, where is the beginning and where is the end? It is the same. It only depends on the the way you want you can look at it. Without free will there is no *karma*. In order to express free will, you need to be born, which is the result of *karma*.

Question: How do the four stages of life recommended by yoga relate to rebirth?

Swami Vishnudevananda: Life starts with the learning period as a child and a teenager. The second stage is the house holder's life, the third stage is the time of retirement, when the children are grown up. Then both husband and wife move out of their home and go to a monastery or a solitary place. As eventually one of the partners will be the first one to die, there is the necessity of a fourth stage of life: the husband and wife live separately like two renounced persons. This is to overcome the attachment which brings unhappiness when either the husband or the wife dies. During this fourth stage you become a swami.

Our present life is a projection of the past, which is temporarily interrupted by death. But when you are reborn in a new body, you will have the same character, the same habits and tendencies. It all came with you in your subconscious mind. Just like today you are doing the same thing as yesterday; you continue to do in this life what you did in the last life. Only if you have a strong will, will you be able to correct your life.

Question: Can a God-realised guru save the *karma* of the disciple?

Swami Vishnudevananda: If any guru says so, please bring him to me so I can prove that he is a hypocrite:

When the guru comes here, tell him that you are going to be his disciple, but that you have a $50,000 debt. Tell that you will be his disciple, therefore could he please take that *karma* of the $50,000 debt away from you. He will not be able to do that.

If you are hungry and the guru eats, what will happen? Nothing—you must eat your own food. It is the same way with *karma*.

If the guru cannot take away your earthly debt, how can he take away your *karmic* debt, which is more powerful than a financial debt? Such a guru is only fooling the student. If he cannot fool you, he will look in another place for a gullible person.

No teacher can take your *karma*. The Teacher must work out his own *karma*. How can he take your *karma*? If anyone says so, he is wrong and really a hypocrite.

Question: Did Christ take the sins away of all humanity?

Swami Vishnudevananda: If Christ took away the sins of all humanity, then during Christ's time no one performed any sins, and no one committed any sin ever after?

If He had taken all the sins away, why were there no saints at that time?

Just imagine if Christ would have taken away all the sins of humanity, why would we have to follow the Ten Commandments? Why would anybody have to follow any rules and regulations?

What Christ did say is "If you abide in my word, you are truly my disciples, and you will know the truth, and the truth will set you free."

Stories

The Story of King Bharata and the Deer

From the *Srimad Bhagavatam*, as told by Swami Vishnudevananda

In ancient days, even the kings would retire to the forest and take *vanaprasta*, the third stage of life. The first stage is *bramacarya*, the learning period, the second is *grihasta*, the house holder's period. When the children are grown up, the property, wealth or country is given to the children and the householders retire to the forest to meditate. This is called *vanaprasta* or entering into *vana*, the forest. Eventually, *sannyasa* is taken, renunciation. The orange robe of swamis is symbolical to demonstrate that they entered the fourth stage.

These are the steps: After the learning period of childhood, school, college, and university comes the householder's period: getting married, raising a family and having a job. When the children are grown up and the job is finished, you retire into the forest and see how you can mold your future life without family attachment. Detaching from wife or husband, children, home, family and money,—that is the most difficult part. When detachment becomes perfect, or when one is at least trying to make it perfect, then comes renunciation. You approach a guru and ask him to initiate you into the order of *sannyasa*, you become a svami or a renunciate. In rare cases, when there is no guru, mental *sannyasa* can be taken by oneself. Some people do it at the last moment of their lives: "I renounce all the pleasures of this world—All the pleasures of the astral world—all the pleasures of the heavenly world."

The great king Bharata renounced his kingdom, all his power and position, and went to the forest. He built a small cottage near the banks of a river, and started doing his daily worship – *mantra japa*, and other *sadhanas* (spiritual practices). He renounced his royal robes, and ate whatever he could find: fruit, roots, leaves. His discipline was very strict. One early morning, before his *puja* or worship, he went to take a bath in the river and saw a deer which had come to drink water. She was fully pregnant. Nearby was a lion the sight of which frightened the deer. She jumped into the flowing river to swim across. As she was pregnant and frightened by the sound of the roaring lion, she gave birth to her baby, which was then carried away by the current.

The king was doing his morning dip in the river and saw the deer baby being washed away. Due to his kind heart and like any other human being would have done, he saved the helpless deer baby and took it to his small cottage. There he started feeding it and took care of it. I once brought up a small squirrel. It wanted to stay with me wherever I went, it came with me for meditation, etc., because I was the only person the squirrel knew. So also, the deer baby became attached to the king and the king got attached to the deer. Slowly the king's mind was captivated by the beautiful, cute deer baby. The king had left the kingdom and had renounced the royal life in the palace. But now the same detached mind became completely immersed in bringing up the deer baby. When the king was meditating and doing pranayama, the deer baby would come and sit quietly next to him. With one eye the king looked at it: "Where are you baby? *OM Namah Sivaya*. Baby, are you ok? *OM Namah Sivaya*. Meditation became a mere ritual, a routine, and the mind moved more and more towards the baby deer. This is how *maya* (illusion) works. When the baby deer goes the king would call, "Where are you, where are you?" The king became old, he reached the final stage of his life. He was lying with heavy fever, unable to sit up and meditate and do his regular *puja*, worship and *pranayama*. Nor could he take care of the deer. But by now the deer was grown up and could take care of itself in the forest. The last thought the king had was not his *mantra OM* or *OM Namah Sivaya* or *OM Namo Narayanaya*. Instead he thought of the baby deer: "Where are you? You didn't come back. Some lion must have killed you. What a pity! I cannot come and help you. Where are you? Come here. Oh my dear baby. I am sick, lying here." Continuously calling the deer, the king left his body. As his last thought was about the deer, in his next life he was born as a deer. Due to his intense practice, he could remember his past life: "What a pity. I renounced my kingdom, my children, my wealth, my property and all my power. I went away, meditated, prayed and worshipped. A deer came, and my mind was diverted towards the deer. What a pity. I lost a great chance. Now I must suffer in this deer body until this deer *karma* is exhausted."

So, with these thoughts, king Bharata wandered in the deer body. As he could not talk in the animal body, he wandered alone, and did not join the other deer. He wandered and waited for the time to drop the deer body. In his next life he was born as a *brahmin* in a highly evolved and religious family. Lord *Kriśna* says that a person who did not reach perfection before the body dies will be reborn in a religious family or even in a family of *jnanis*, people who have attained God realization like our Master Śivananda.

Bharata, the previous king, who had spent one lifetime as a deer, now changed into a *brahmin* costume, as a son of a very pious *brahmin* family. The father died very early, so Bharata was brought up by an elder brother. After experiencing the consequences of attachment to the deer, Bharata decided that in this life he would not get attached to anybody or anything. From the very beginning the young boy acted as dumb and deaf. If other *brahmin* boys would do *pranayama*, take an early morning bath or play, he would not join them. He acted as a mad boy, unable to learn, unable to study. Yet he had the complete inner knowledge. "*Āham Brahmasmi*" – "I am the Absolute" was burning inside constantly, he lived in the awareness of the *ātman* or the indwelling divinity. External things were not important for him. Rituals were meaningless, he had done them all in his previous life. He pretended to be stupid, an idiot, so that he would not get attracted to anybody and no one would love him. Detachment was natural for him from childhood.

As his brothers had to feed him, they gave him the job to sit in the field to drive away the crows and other birds which came to eat the grain. He was very happy, as he could sit and meditate in the field, and food was provided for him. He was thinking only of the *ātman*, he was constantly in meditation, in the atmic bliss, but acted as fool. He became a very strong young man and didn't care about anything except that one *ātman*, seeing one God everywhere.

One day the wife of a king of thieves gave birth to a son. This thief was a very ferocious and evil man and would kill anybody for anything. He prayed to mother *Kali*, the divine mother in a negative form, to be blessed with a son: "If I have a son, I will give you an offering of a human head." By the grace of the mother, a son was born to him, and he had to keep his promise to sacrifice the head of a human being. His thieves saw in the middle of the field a very healthy and strong man. "Our *Badrakali*", the deity they were praying to, "will love this animal. A perfect *prasad* for *Kali*." They took him away, but he did not care, it made no difference to him. He was taken in front of the *Kali* temple. In preparation of the sacrifice, his body was bathed, oiled and scented with sandal paste and red powder. Then he was brought to the sacrificial altar in front of the Kali statue. The priest came and chanted the *Kali mantras* before cutting his head off.

He had neither hate nor fear towards anybody, as he was beyond all duality and lived constantly in *Brahman*. This powerful inner *brahmic* fire started burning *Kali* herself, she could not bear that universal power, the spiritual heat coming from the *brahmin*. She came out of the statue and took her real *Kali* form. She took the sword and cut the heads of all thieves. He looked at it and bowed to the mother as an expression of the one Divinity who had manifested in the form of *Kali* to destroy the negative forces. Then he walked away.

But *karma* was not over. As he was walking, he met a big royal procession. King *Rahugan* was going to see his teacher to receive initiation. In the olden days the king was carried in a palanquin with all paraphernalia, drums, kettles, flutes and so forth. One of the palanquin bearers was limping due to an injury and could not carry the king anymore. As they saw this young neatly dressed *brahmin*, he was told to carry the royal palanquin. As he was now walking under the palanquin, he saw an ant colony moving across the path. He didn't want to step on any ant and so he jumped. The palanquin was shaking and the king shouted angrily, "What is happening there?" and the captain warned him, "Be careful. The king is there. Walk properly. March 1,2. 1,2. Left right, left right." Then he saw a frog on the way. So he stopped suddenly and caused a sudden break. The king became impatient, came out of the palanquin and took his sword. "Don't you know who am I? I am the king and I can give life and death to you". Now for the first time in his life King Bharata opened his mouth, after having acted as deaf and dumb all this time. He addressed the king, who was an evolved person, ready to receive a spiritual initiation: "Oh King you said that you can give life or death? But you can only kill this body. The *ātman* within me cannot be touched by you or by anything." The king was shocked. This was clearly not an ordinary man, though he appeared to be a fool. He spoke words of a *jnani*, a knower of *Vedanta*. Bharata continued, "This body is made up of food. You can only cut this body and the body will go eventually back to earth or ashes. Your body also, oh king, will one day go to earth or into ashes though you are sitting in the palanquin."

The king fell at his feet. Who are you? Are you Dattatreya, the great sage? Or Dakśinamurti? Who are you? Are you a great siddha?" Now king Bharata knew that this king was fit to be initiated and that his mind was ready. He said, "I was a king like you and people would carry me. Due to my attachment, I became a deer, because my last thought was with the deer. Then because of my past remembrance I was born as a *brahmin*. But I didn't do the rituals like other *brahmin* boys and I acted as if I was dumb and deaf. Now for the first time I opened my mouth." Eventually he initiated the king into the greatest knowledge: *Ṭat Ṭvam Āsi*. That Thou art. You are not the king, you are not the kingly body. This body is like a cloth you are wearing. You change your costume but the *ātman*, the reality, the soul, is ever living in you. Meditate on the soul." After the initiation king Bharata left and continued his life. As a jnani he never stayed in any place. He attained the ultimate reality, God.

This is the story of Bharata. Even after having reached a very high state, you still can fall and can go back into lower wombs, an animal womb or even a plant womb. If you practice *japa* then your last thought will be God, not the nurses and doctors poking you with intravenous feeding, putting you in a wheel chair, taking you to the operation theatre for organ transplant. Would you prefer to extend your physical life in this way, or learn to bring the *prana* up to the second, third, fourth, fifth, sixth and seventh level? Or at least you can remember how to inhale and to exhale with the repetition of *OM* and experience the silence. That positive silence is God. Now you are in a blissful state, everlasting peace. You merge in the supreme *atmic* bliss of God.

This body is created by *karma* and there will be pain and disease, no number of healers or medical doctors can change that. The king became a deer. That is negative *karma* and he has to carry the king. He was even taken to the *Kali* temple. But he transcended the duality and went beyond the fear of death.

I saw a CBS documentary: a person was brought in a terminal condition to the emergency ward. His family members asked the doctors what they were going to do.

"We do all the tests we need to do."

"How long the person will live?"

"Maybe 24 hours, maybe less."

"Then why are you taking all the tests."
"We have to do our duty."

Emergency ward, then X-ray ward, next some blood tests, and many more expensive tests. The CBS television camera television followed the patient until all tests were completed. The patient died, but the cost of the tests during the last 20 hours of his life amounted to $40.000.

So CBS was asking why all these things had been done. The hospital management replied "Who is going to pay for all these expensive machines? So we have to charge the patients. Plus if you don't do all these tests, we might be sued for malpractice, for not taking proper care of the patients."

The patient did not survive and the last moment of his life were filled with fear and and a painful condition. He could not even see his relatives. Anyway the family might have asked questions like: where are the insurance papers? Where did you keep the money? What is written in the will? Then his last thought would have been, "They are only interested in the will." And in the next life, the same story will start all over again: the child grows up, gets married, has children and grandchildren and much attachment. The same situation as before, just with a different costume.

A Worm speaks on the Conquest of Death

From the Mahabharata
as presented by Swami Sivananda

Yudhiṣthira:
1. "Wishing to die and wishing to live, many persons surrender their lives in the great sacrifice (of battle). Tell me, O grandfather, what is the end that these attain to?
2—3. "To give up life in battle is fraught with sorrow for men. O you of great wisdom, you know that to give up life is difficult for men, whether they are rich or poor, or are in happiness or misery. In my opinion, you are gifted with omniscience. Do tell me the reason of this."

Bhiśma said:
4. "In prosperity or adversity, in weal or woe, living creatures, O king, coming into this world, live according to a particular method.
5. "Listen to me as I explain the reason to you. The question you have put to me is, indeed, excellent, O Yudhiṣthira!
6. "Regarding it, O king, I shall explain to you the old dialogue that took place between the Dvaipayana Riśi and a crawling worm.
7. "Formerly when the learned *brahmana*, viz., the Kriśna Dvaipayana, having identified himself with *Brahman*, roamed over the world, he saw on a road over which carts used to pass, a worm moving quickly.
8. "The Rishi knew the course of every creature and the language of every animal. Gifted with omniscience, he addressed the worm in these words:
9. "O worm, you appear to be greatly alarmed, and to be in great haste. Tell me, where do you run, and whence have you been afraid?"

The worm said:

10. "I am stricken with fear on hearing the rattle of that large cart. O you! of great intelligence, it makes a fearful roar. It is almost come.

11. "The sound is heard. Will it not kill me? I am flying away from this. I hear the sound of the bulls.

12. "They are breathing hard under the whip of the driver, as they are carrying the heavy load. I hear also the various sounds made by the men who are driving the bulls.

13. "Creatures like us born as worms, cannot bear such sounds. It is, therefore, that I am flying from this situation of great fright.

14. "Death is considered by all creatures as painful. Life is an acquisition difficult to make. Hence I fly away in fear, I do not wish to pass from a state of weal to one of woe."

Bhiṣma said:

15. "Thus addressed, Dvaipayana Vyasa said: 'O worm, whence can be your happiness? You belong to the intermediate order of being. I think, death would be of happiness to you.

16. "Sound, touch, taste, scent and various kinds of excellent enjoyments are unknown to you, O worm! I think death will prove a benefit to you'."

The worm said:

17. "A living creature however circumstanced it may be, becomes attached to it. Even in this order of being I am happy, I think, O you of great wisdom! It is for this that I wish to live.

18. "In this condition, every object of enjoyment exists for me according to the necessity of my body. Human beings and those creatures which originate from immobile objects have different enjoyments.

19. "In my former life I was a human being, O powerful one. I was a wealthy *śudra*. I was not devoted to the *brahmanas*. I was cruel, vile in conduct, and an usurer.

20. "I was harsh in speech. I considered cunningness as wisdom. I hated all creatures. Taking advantage of pretexts in agreements made between myself and others, I used always to take away what belonged to others.

21. "Without feeding servants and guests who came to my home, I used to fill, when hungry, my own stomach, proud, greedy of good food, cruel as I was.

22. "Covetous as I was of riches, I never dedicated with faith and respect any food to the celestials and the departed manes, although duty enjoined me to dedicate food to them.

23. "Those men who moved by fear came to me for seeking my help, I sent them adrift without giving any protection. I did not extend my help to those who came to me with prayers for removing their fear.

24. "I used to feel unreasonable envy at seeing other people's riches, and corn, and wives held dear by them and articles of drink, and good palaces.

25. "Seeing the happiness of others, I was filled with envy and I always wished them poverty. Acting thus which promised to crown my own wishes with fruition, I sought to destroy the virtue, riches and pleasures of other people.

26. "In the past life of mine, I committed various deeds moved by cruelty and such other passions. Recollecting those deeds, I am filled with repentance and grief, as one is filled with grief at the loss of his dear son.

27. "On account of those deeds of mine, I do not know what the fruits of good deeds are. I, however, adored my old mother and on one occasion adored a *brahmana*.

28. "Gifted with birth and accomplishments, that *brahmana*, while travelling, came to my house once as a guest. I received him with respectful hospitality. On account of the merit of that deed my memory has not forsaken me.

29. "I think that on account of that deed I shall once more succeed in regaining happiness."

(*Ānusasanika Parva—Mahabharata*)

Rebirth – A Record of some Interesting Cases

A collection presented by Swami Sivananda

Soldier Castor, the Burmese speaker—George Castor, related some of his past experiences in the Sunday Express, London, (1935). He was a soldier born in 1889. From his boyhood he was speaking while asleep in Burmese. In 1907 he joined the army. In 1909 when he was 20, he was transferred to Maymyo (Burma) and there he felt that he had seen the land, lived in it, spoken the Burmese tongue, known the Irrawaddy and he told Lance Corporal Carrigon that on the other side of the Irrawaddy, there was a large temple with a huge crack in the wall from top to bottom and nearby a large bell—a statement that was found true to the letter.

An 18 year old boy of Jhamapukhur (Calcutta) was on his death-bed. The boy's parents had thrown themselves at the feet of a ṣadhu puruṣa but, at the same time, had tried other means for the boy's cure. The aunt of the boy blamed the ṣadhu puruṣa saying that faith in the ṣadhu was killing him. At this the boy burst out:

"The ṣadhu puruṣa is not to blame. You could not put your trust in him. What has befallen me is nothing, when my past *karma* is considered. A thousand times more should I suffer. In my past life, I worked in a Railway office and murdered a person, I cut him to pieces. Oh! how I pained him. Where will that *karma* go?

"All this happened about 50 years ago when the Suke Street Thana was in charge of a reputed officer who was known as 'Kana' sergeant as he was blind in one eye. He succeeded in arresting me, I escaped the gallows but got hard labour."

Then addressing his mother the boy said: "Mother, I am going now. Do you know why? The person who is sleeping in the other room (referring to his father) was my son in my last birth. He did all he could to make me miserable. To make him feel the consequence of his past *karma* I am now born as his son. He must now himself feel the pain and sorrow a son can inflict on his father. *Karma* can never be evaded and must always be endured."

(Enquiry showed that Suke Street Thana was actually in charge of an officer who was famous all over the city as the blind sergeant and who retired about 50 years ago).

Hill, the South American explorer—Mr. Hill writes to the Editor of the 'People': "I had a strong belief that certain parts of South America were familiar to me. I had a recurring dream that I was an explorer wandering alone in a tropical forest when suddenly a band of dark-skinned men appeared to whom I spoke in their tongue. But for some reason they became angry and their leaders struck me.

Eventually, I became a steward in the Royal Mail Liners and went to South America. There, I found myself anticipating the names of obscure streets and buildings with accuracy, and I felt as I made my way about Rio de Janeiro, Santos and Buenos Aires that I had surely walked there before. On one voyage we took on board a Danish author at Santos. One day he sent for me to come to his cabin, and said: 'Steward, you are the victim of a remarkable coincidence or something far stranger.'

"Then he showed me a human head taken by him from the head-hunters of Amazon, reduced by a secret process to half of its normal size and preserved. I shuddered. I know I was looking at an exact counterpart of my own face."

Bajitpur Postal Clerk's Son (Advance 15 Jul. 1936)—a three year-old son of a postal clerk of Bajitpur (Faridpur) began to cry one day and insisted on going to his own home. In reply to a question, he said:

"I am an inhabitant of Fazilpur in Chittagong. From Luxum Railway Station a road leads to my village. I have three sons and four daughters there. The Kalibari of Meher is not very far off from my residence. It is at the Meher Kalibari that Sarvananda realised salvation. There is no image of There is a big banyan tree and worship is held at its root."

There is also a very tall palm tree. The father of the boy had never been to Chittagong or Luxum station or to Meher Kalibari. The boy sometimes sings songs which he had never heard.

A Hungarian girl forgets her parents—in 1933, a 15-year-old Hungarian daughter of an engineer lay on her deathbed at Budapest. Apparently she died, but recovered a little later, forgot her native Hungarian language completely and began to speak Spanish only. She could not recognise even her parents whom she referred to as: "These nice people here are very kind to me, but they are not my parents as they pretend to be." To a Spanish interpreter, she said: "I am Senora Lucid Attarez de Salvio. I was the wife of a working man in Madrid and had 14 children. I was 40 years old and rather sick. A few years ago I died, at least thought I was dying. Now I have recovered in this strange country."

She is singing Spanish songs, preparing special Spanish food and giving graphic descriptions of Madrid where she has never been.

Jung Bahadur's daughter (Delhi)—Shanta, an 8-year old girl of Lala Jung Bahadur, a merchant of Delhi, used to say, ever since she could talk—that in her former life she was married to a man of Mathura whose address she gave. When her former husband was informed of it, he sent his brother whom the girl identified instantly. Then her husband came and she recognised him at once, and told him facts which were known only to him and his former wife. She also told him that she had buried one hundred rupees at a certain place in her home.

Devi Prasad's child, Kanpur (Āmrita Bazar Patrika 1 May 1938)—A five-year-old child of one Devi Prasad Bhatnagar, living in Premnagar, Kanpur, says that in his previous birth his name was Sivadayal Muktas and that he had been murdered during the Kanpur riots in 1931 when he was decoyed by two Muslim friends to a house and there murdered. One day the child insisted on going to his old house where he said his former wife was lying ill. He was taken there and he at once recognised his wife, his children and other articles.

Recites the Gita at one year and a half—correspondent from Prayagraj reports (A.B. Patrika):

"A three-year-old boy at Jhansi can reproduce from memory the whole Srimad Bhagavadgita and Ramayana and his pronunciation is perfect. The boy was trying in vain to speak something since he attained the age of 5 months and at the age of one year and a half he recited to his hearers the Gita, etc."

A five-year-old child and Piano (People 20 Jun. 1937)—A five-year-old Blackpool child would rather play the Piano than play with a doll. She has never had a lesson, yet she plays brilliantly. She can play in perfect tune any melody she hears and she adds a tune or two of her own composition.

Barrister's daughter (Calcutta)—The daughter of a barrister of the Calcutta High Court, when only 3 years old, could clean the house floors excellently. On being asked she said:

"I used to clean the floors in my father-in-law's house in Beldanga where only myself, my father-in-law and one of his daughters lived. I used to perform *puja* and cook Thakurji's Bhog (offering to Lord Krishna). There was a Dole Mancha in my father-in-law's house. On the Dole Yatra Day we used to put Thakurji (Lord Krishna) on a swing and smear him profusely with Avir (holy paste)."

The child lives in strict *ācara* (religious discipline) and does not eat or sleep with her parents who are anglicised and therefore untouchables. Her food is separately cooked.

These facts can be easily verified even now.

With strongest ties to the earth, with desires and affections hovering over earthly scenes, the generality of persons are reborn on earth, immediately after death. They do not sojourn in other planes of existence. Some of them, as it happens, though rarely, remember their immediate past incarnation. Here are two from the many cases published in the *Fate* magazine, in the year 1954.

Anne, aged four, said to her father: "Daddy, I have been here on earth lots of times."

When he laughed, Anne became indignant. "I was! I was! I was!" she cried, stamping her foot, "Once I went to Canada as a man. I remember my name even. It was Lishus Faber. I was a soldier and I took the gates!"

After months of research, a historian found the evidence of a battle in Canada in which a single soldier had "taken the gates" as Anne had said.

The name of the lieutenant was Aloysius La-Febre—Lishus Faber as pronounced by Anne.

Visvanath, born in Bareilly, began at the age of three to give minute details of a previous life in a town called Pilibhit. His parents, fearing that this meant he was going to die young did their best to conceal their son's story.

The boy named the school to which he had gone in Pilibhit in his previous existence and said they had a neighbour named Lala Sunder Lal who had a green gate, a sword and he described the parties which this wealthy man had given.

To test him the boy was taken to this distant town, which he had never visited before in his present life. Here he correctly pointed out various parts of his original home, now in ruins, including a hidden stairway. Shown a group photograph, he correctly pointed out a man as his former uncle, Har Narain, and finally pointed to himself—a boy sitting amidst the group.

Every detail was found to be correct. His own identity was established as Laxmi Narain, who had died of tuberculosis at the age of 32.

Laxmi Narain's mother was still living. She asked little Visvanath numerous questions to test his memory. He answered every question correctly without a moment's hesitation.

Strange Case of Transmigration of a Soul

MORADABAD, August 23.—Quite a sensation has been caused following the arrival here on August 15 of a boy named Pramod from Bisauli, district Badaun, who revealed the incidents of his previous life which were found accurate to the minutest detail. Thousands of people, including several prominent figures of the city, visited him during the two days of his stay here and a clear case of transmigration of soul was established in the end.

The boy, aged five and a half years, said that he was Parama Nand, brother of B. Mohanlal, Proprietor of the renowned catering Firm of Messers. Mohan Brothers, having branches in Saharanpur and Moradabad, and he died at Saharanpur on May 9, 1943, following a chronic pain in the stomach.

Born at Bisauli on March 15, 1944, just nine months and six days after the death of Parama Nand, as son of Babu Bankey Lal Sharma Shastri, M.A., Professor in Inter College, Bisauli, the boy as early as he could pronounce the words, uttered clearly the name of Mohan, Moradabad and Saharanpur, and later also pronounced the words Mohan Brothers. Whenever he saw his relations purchasing biscuits and butter he said he had a big biscuit factory in Moradabad. Whenever he saw big shops in the market he said that his shop in Moradabad was bigger than any other shop. He used to insist on his parents now and then to take him to Moradabad. The name of the boy as entered in his *Janma Kundali* (horoscope) by the *Pundits* was also Paramanand, a strange coincidence, but the name of his elder brother being Varmod, he also began to be called as Parmod. But the child always insisted that he was Parama Nand, that he had his brothers, sons, daughter and wife at Moradabad.

Mohan Lal Moves

It so happened that early this year, one Lala Raghunandan Lal of Bisauli told one of his relatives living in Moradabad about the boy and his assertions regarding his relationship with the Mohan Brothers. Thereupon, the relations concerned told the whole story to Sri Mohanlal, the proprietor of the firm. Sri Mohanlal, together with some of his relatives, visited Bisauli last July and met the boy's father. The boy was, however, away in some distant village with some of his relatives and therefore could not be seen. Sri Mohanlal requested Prof. Bankey Lal to bring the boy to Moradabad and the request was acceded. It was promised that the professor would bring the boy to Moradabad during the forthcoming Independence Day Holidays.

On August 15, on alighting from the train, the boy at once recognised his brother and embraced him. On the way from the station to the residence of Sri Mohanlal the boy recognised the Town Hall and said that his shop was now near at hand. When the tonga was by-passing the shop, as arranged, in order to test the boy, he at once asked the tonga to be stopped before the shop of Mohan Brothers. Then he stepped towards the house situated in front of the shop and got into the room where the late Parama Nand used to keep his articles of worship and cash box.

On entering the room he bowed in salutation. It was a very pathetic scene when he recognised his former wife and other relations and recalled several incidents of his past life which concerned them. All agreed that the incidents were true. The boy could not, however, recognise his former eldest son, now 17 years, who was only 13 when Parama Nand died. When the boy recalled that all the brothers used to sit together and drink lemons, etc., all the brothers and others present began to weep.

The Soda Machine
The boy then expressed his desire to go to his "gaddi" and on entering the shop went to the soda machine and explained the process of manufacturing aerated water, a thing which he had never seen in his present life. He told that the water connection had been stopped, as it had really been done in order to test his memory.

The boy then expressed his wish to go to Victory Hotel, owned by Sri Karam Chand, a cousin of Parama Nand. He led the way to the building and to the upper storey and at once exclaimed that the rooms at present constructed on the roof were not there before.

Sahu Nandlal Saran, the premier citizen of Moradabad, took the boy in his car to the Meston Park, and asked him to locate the place where his civil lines branch had once been. He thereupon led the company to the Gujarati Building, owned by Sahu Nandlal Saran, and pointed out the shop where once the branch of Mohan Brothers had been. On his way to the Meston Park the boy recognised the Allahabad Bank, Water Works and District Jail.

It may be noted that throughout his excursions to the different places in the city, done either to fulfil his wish to see places connected with his past life or to test his memory, a large number of persons were present and it was a sight worth seeing. Everybody was moved. The boy recognised several other places and persons who used to visit the shop during his past life.

At the Public Meeting

A large public meeting was held on August 16 at the Arya Samaj where the boy's father, Prof. Bankey Lal, explained the development of the boy's memory since his childhood.

It was with great difficulty that the boy was taken back from Moradabad. As he was not willing to go away from his old relations and the shop, he was carried away in the early hours of August 17 while asleep.

A deep impression has been created upon those gentlemen here who do not believe either in God or in the transmigration of soul. As a gentleman told me, "No explanation is necessary for those who believe, no explanation is possible for those who do not."

There is no need to mention that neither the boy nor his father ever visited Moradabad previously. The tone, the unhesitating manner and the correctness of details narrated by him were found to be absolutely fool-proof and not even once did he falter.

About twelve years ago, a similar, rather more remarkable event took place in Delhi, when Śanti Devi, aged nine years, was taken to Mathura where she identified her former husband, her house and many other details connected with her previous life.

—"Āmrita Bazar Patrika", Aug., 1949.

A Well-Known Case Of Rebirth—Śanti Devi

A sensational, sensational because so amazingly credible, and true case of rebirth at Delhi, reported officially by a locally appointed committee consisting of enlightened, critical and competent men, was much publicised in leading Indian and foreign newspapers. Born on the 12th October, 1926, Śanti Devi, a little girl, who bore in her memory the most vivid and living pictures of the whole span of her past life beginning in the year 1902 and ending in the year 1925, began ever since she could speak, to recollect and narrate whenever the context and associations in daily life necessitated, the incidents, events and experiences in surprising detail of her past life at Mathura with her husband Pundit Kedar Nath Chaubey. Her unbelieving parents not only dismissed such graphic narrations of the past life, as though they were the jabber of a child, but fervently hoped that these recollections would efface themselves from the memory of the child as she grew. But, contrary to their expectation and hope, the child was insistent on recollecting more and yet more of her past life, and persisted in requesting her parents to take her to Mathura the city of her previous birth, where she desired to show the present parents, her old house and certain things in it which only an inmate who long lived in it could have so done.

At last, the child prevailed over the parents. A grand uncle of the girl was called; Śanti Devi gave him the address of her husband in her previous life; inquiries were made; communication was sent to her husband Pundit Kedar Nath and surprisingly enough a response came from Pundit Kedar Nath of Mathura who in his letter, among other things, suggested to the inquiring party at Delhi, to contact a relation of his, Pundit Kanji Mal of Delhi, and give him an interview with the child, Śanti Devi. No sooner Sri Kanji Mal was brought into her presence, she had not only recognised him to be the younger cousin of her husband but made most satisfactory response to the other question touching facts of an intimate nature.

Aroused to a fresh and active interest in efforts at probing into the facts of Śanti Devi's narration of the events, facts and experiences of her past life, the parents, the party and Kanji Mal called Kedar Nath Chaubey to Delhi, from Mathura. When Pundit Kedar Nath Chaubey came to Delhi, with his ten-year old son, and his present wife, to see Śanti Devi, at the very first sight, Śanti Devi recognised her husband and felt greatly touched by the figure of her son, and began to shed tears. After a long interchange of thought and words between Śanti Devi and her alleged husband, who was greatly moved by the veracity of the recollections and the truth of her statements, Pundit Kedar Nath confirmed the fact that this was the same soul, viz., that of his first wife who had died at Mathura, and stated that her narration of the details in each of their particulars was true. This made the parents grant the repeated request that the girl Śanti Devi made many a time during the past few years, to go to Mathura, which the girl now reiterated with greater force as a result of the present meeting with her husband of her previous life. Śanti Devi not only gave out the colour of the house at Mathura, named the roads and streets leading to that house, described the Visram Ghat, the temple of Dwarkadish, but stated certain things which only the former wife of Pundit Kedar Nath could alone have known. She also said that she had hidden "underground" in the upper-storey room of the house at Mathura, some money, a hundred rupees from which she had vowed to give to the temple of Dwarakadhish.

Upon the grant of this request and wish of Śanti Devi to go to Mathura, the persuasion of the investigating committee was exerted; and the party with the committee, parents and Śanti Devi, left for Mathura. As the train steamed into the Mathura station, Śanti Devi shouted in joy, "Mathura has come", "Mathura has come", and when she got down from the train, identifying in the crowd an elderly man wearing a typical Mathura dress, whom she had never met before, she came down from the arms of Deshbandhu Gupta where she was, and instinctively touched the feet of the old man stating that he was the elder brother of her husband named Babu Ram Chaubey. This fact when found to be true, was but only one among the many surprises that Śanti Devi held for the admiration and awe for her witnesses. She had not only led the way to the house at Mathura, from the Railway station, but went on giving certain interesting facts as that there was on that particular road no tar earlier, and when once in the house of her description, she had successfully passed every test that the inquiring gentleman put to her.

When she was taken to the pilgrims guest house at Mathura, she identified the 'brother' of her previous birth, now in twenties, and recognised her 'uncle-in-law'. At every step the truth of her past narrations which were dismissed as so much of a child's jabberings were proved true beyond doubt. When in the house of her description, she entered its courtyard and felt dismayed at the absence of the well that was there during her previous incarnation, noting which her husband Pundit Kedar Nath lifted up the stone covering the wall-less well and showed her the well. And going upstairs, she dug up the hole where she had hidden her money, and to her uneasiness the money was not there, as it was, as Pundit Kedar Nath confessed that he had taken it from there, after the death of his former wife, now the girl Santi Devi. After this when she was taken to her parents' house, she recognised them, and both the girl and the parents sank into continued sobs; it was with great difficulty that the girl was weaned away from the parents of her previous birth, and taken to the Visram Ghat where she unfolded many more surprises to the investigating committee and to others by the display of the contents of the memories of her previous life. Such instances as these are not uncommon in India. There was also another case of a girl who recognised her parents of her previous birth, and when a similar process of investigation was conducted, and her narrations found true, the parents of the girl in her previous life, who were rich began to support her, and give her a decent education, as the later parents were poor. It is ridiculous to presume that rebirth is untrue when one has not taken pains to pursue the results of the investigations that have been conducted.

Tap the Source

www.sivananda.org

Sivananda Yoga Retreat House, Tyrol, Austria

Join us at a **Sivananda Yoga Vedanta Centre and Ashram** to recharge, reconnect, and transform your life through classical yoga and meditation:

The Sivananda Centers offer
- daily yoga classes which combine postures, breathing, and relaxation to build strength, flexibility, longevity and inner calm. The practice is suitable for all levels.
- group meditations inspire peace and joy through silent practice, chanting, and uplifting spiritual talks.
- nutrition and cooking courses promote simple wholesome vegetarian meals that nourish body and mind.
- lectures and workshops on stress management, meditation, and yoga philosophy share time-tested practical wisdom.

The Sivananda Ashrams offer

Year-round programs on health, peace and self-realization through the practice and teaching of classical yoga.

Sivananda Yoga Vacation
Relax. Rebalance. Reconnect.

Take a meaningful break in a peaceful ashram setting with the Sivananda Yoga Vacation Program. Open to all levels, this program offers a balanced blend of yoga, meditation, and spiritual learning in a supportive, natural environment.
- Daily yoga classes and guided meditation
- Inspiring talks on yoga philosophy and wellness
- Two wholesome vegetarian meals per day
- Free time to rest, reflect, or explore nature

Whether you're new to yoga or a seasoned practitioner, this retreat helps restore energy, deepen self-awareness, and bring lasting peace into your daily life.

The Sivananda Yoga Teachers' Training Course – TTC:

This renowned four-week residential program was founded by Swami Vishnudevananda in 1969 and offers an immersive experience in traditional **classical yoga**. It is designed for both dedicated yoga practitioners and aspiring teachers who wish to deepen their personal practice and share yoga's holistic teachings.

The course provides a balanced blend of theory, practice, and spiritual study, covering:
- **Asanas (yoga postures)** – systematic practice and correction of the 12 basic postures and their variations.
- **Pranayama (breathing techniques)** – instruction in classical breathing exercises for vitality and mental clarity.

- **Meditation and mantra chanting** – development of concentration, inner peace, and spiritual awareness.
- **A lacto-vegetarian diet** based on the principles of ahimsa (non-violence) and its positive effects on body and mind.
- **Yoga philosophy and psychology** – study of the Bhagavad Gita, Vedanta, and the teachings of Swami Sivananda.
- **Anatomy and physiology** – understanding the physical and energetic effects of yoga practices.
- **Karma Yoga (selfless service)** – integrating yoga into daily life through service and community participation.

Students follow a **structured daily routine**, beginning early with meditation, chanting, and classes, maintaining silence during certain hours, and observing a vegetarian diet that supports yogic living.

Upon successful completion, participants receive the **Yoga Siromani (Teacher of Yoga)** certification, recognized by the **Sivananda Yoga Vedanta Centres** and affiliated with **Yoga Alliance (RYT 200)**. Graduates leave with the tools, discipline, and inspiration to teach and live yoga as a way of life.

Advanced Sivananda Yoga Teachers' Training Course (ATTC)

This four-week intensive program builds upon the foundation of the Sivananda TTC, offering a deeper study of classical yoga. It expands understanding of **Vedanta philosophy, Raja Yoga,** and the **subtle aspects of yoga practice.**

The course includes advanced training in **asanas, pranayama, meditation,** and **mantra chanting,** along with in-depth study of **the Yoga Sutras of Patanjali.** Students also explore **advanced anatomy** to refine their teaching and personal practice, as well as an introduction to reading writing **Sanskrit**.

Conducted in a disciplined ashram setting, the ATTC emphasizes self-transformation through **study, practice, and service**. Graduates are awarded the **Yoga Acharya (Master of Yoga)** certification, internationally recognized by the **Sivananda Yoga Vedanta Centres** and **Yoga Alliance (RYT 500)**.

Sivananda Yoga Sadhana Intensive Course

This is a rigorous two-week advanced program designed by **Swami Vishnudevananda** for experienced yoga practitioners and graduates of the Sivananda TTC. Rooted in the traditional teachings of **Swami Sivananda**, it focuses on deepening personal **sadhana (spiritual practice)** through intensive **pranayama, advanced asanas**, and **meditation**. The course emphasizes mastery of classical **Hatha Yoga techniques,** including extended pranayama sessions, cleansing practices, and in-depth study of **yogic scriptures** such as the Hatha Yoga Pradipika as well as an introduction to the Srimad Bhagavatam and the Viveka Chudamani.

Conducted in a retreat-style ashram environment with a disciplined routine, the Sadhana Intensive aims to purify the body and mind, strengthen concentration, and elevate spiritual awareness. It offers a transformative experience for dedicated practitioners seeking to internalize the teachings of yoga and advance on the path of self-realization.

Sivananda Yoga Vedanta Ashrams and Centres

Ashrams

Sivananda Ashram Yoga Camp
673 8th Avenue, Val Morin
Québec, J0T 2R0, CANADA
hq@sivananda.org
www.sivanandacanada.org/camp/

Sivananda Ashram Yoga Ranch
P.O. Box 195, 500 Budd Road
Woodbourne, NY 12788,
UNITED STATES
yogaranch@sivananda.org
www.sivanandayogaranch.org/

Sivananda Ashram Yoga Retreat
P.O. Box N 7550 Paradise Island,
Nassau, BAHAMAS
nassau@sivananda.org
www.sivanandabahamas.org/

Sivananda Yoga Vedanta Dhanwantari Ashram
P.O. Neyyar Dam,
Dt. Thiruvananthapuram, Kerala
695 572, INDIA
guestindia@sivananda.org
www.sivananda.org.in/neyyardam

Sivananda Ashram Yoga Farm
14651 Ballantree Lane, Comp. 8
Grass Valley, California CA 95949,
UNITED STATES
yogafarm@sivananda.org
www.sivanandayogafarm.org/

Sivananda Yoga Vedanta Meenakshi Ashram
(near Pavana Vilakku Junction)
New Natham Road, Saramthangi
Village, Vellayampatti P.O. Madurai
Dt., Tamil Nadu 625 503, INDIA
madurai@sivananda.org
www.sivananda.org.in/madurai

Sivananda Kutir (near Siror Bridge)
P.O. Netala, Uttara Kashi District,
Uttaranchal, Himalayas 249193,
INDIA
himalayas@sivananda.org
www.sivananda.org.in/uttarkashi/

Sivananda Yoga Retreat House
Bichlach 40, 6370 Reith near
Kitzbühel, AUSTRIA
tyrol@sivananda.net
www.sivananda.at

Ashram de Yoga Sivananda
26 Impasse du Bignon,
45170 Neuville-aux-Bois, FRANCE
orleans@sivananda.net
www.sivanandaorleans.org

Sivananda Yoga Vietnam Resort and Training Center
K'Lan Resort,Hoa Hong Street,
Ward 4, Tuyen Lam Lake
Da Lat City, Lam Dong Province
VIETNAM
vietnamyogaresort@sivananda.org
www.sivanandayogavietnam.org

Sivananda Yoga Vedanta
Tapaswini Ashram
Guthavaripalem, Kadivedu P.O.,
Chilakur Mandalam, Gudur,
Tirupati DT.,
Andhra Pradesh 524410, INDIA
gudur@sivananda.org
www.sivananda.org.in/gudur/

Centres

AUSTRIA

Sivananda Yoga Vedanta Zentrum
Prinz-Eugen-Straße 18
1040 Vienna
vienna@sivananda.net
www.wien.sivananda.yoga

CANADA

Sivananda Yoga Vedanta Centre
77 Harbord Street
Toronto, Ontario, M5S 1G4
toronto@sivananda.org
www.sivanandacanada.org/toronto

FRANCE

Centre Sivananda de Yoga
Vedanta
140 Rue du Faubourg Saint-Martin
75010 Paris
paris@sivananda.net
www.sivanandaparis.org

GERMANY

Sivananda Yoga Vedanta Zentrum
Luisenstraße 45
80333 Munich
munich@sivananda.net
www.muenchen.sivananda.yoga

Sivananda Yoga Vedanta Zentrum
Schmiljanstraße 24
12161 Berlin
berlin@sivananda.net
www.berlin.sivananda.yoga

INDIA

Sivananda Yoga Vedanta Nataraja Centre
A-41 Kailash Colony,
New Delhi 110 048
delhi@sivananda.org
www.sivananda.org.in/delhi

Sivananda Yoga Vedanta Dwarka Centre
PSP Pocket, Sector – 6 (near DAV school, next to Kamakshi Apts)
Swami Sivananda Marg, Dwarka,
New Delhi 110 075
dwarka@sivananda.org
www.sivananda.org.in/dwarka

Sivananda Yoga Vedanta Centre
TC 37/1927 (5), Airport Road, West Fort P.O. Thiruvananthapuram,
Kerala 695 023
trivandrum@sivananda.org
www.sivananda.org.in/trivandrum

Sivananda Yoga Vedanta Centre
3/655, Kuppam Road, Kaveri Nagar, Kottivakkam, Chennai,
Tamil Nadu 600 041
chennai@sivananda.org
www.sivananda.org.in/chennai

ISRAEL

Sivananda Yoga Vedanta Centre
6 Lateris Street, Tel Aviv 64166
telaviv@sivananda.org
www.sivananda.co.il

JAPAN

Sivananda Yoga Center
Funabashi 4-21-3, Setagaya-ku,
Tokyo, 156-0055
tokyo@sivananda.org
www.sivanandajp.org

Shojiko Retreat
789 Shoji, Fujikawaguchiko-machi,
Minamitsuru-gun,
Yamanashi-Ken, 401-0336
shojikoretreat@sivananda.jp
www.sivanandajp.org/shojikoretreat

LITHUANIA

Sivananda Jogos Vedantos Centras
Pamėnkalnio g. 28-2
Vilnius 01114
vilnius@sivananda.net
www.sivananda.lt

SPAIN

Centro de Yoga Sivananda Vedanta
Calle Eraso 4
28028 Madrid
madrid@sivananda.net
www.sivananda.es

SWITZERLAND

Centre Sivananda de Yoga Vedanta
1 Rue des Minoteries
1205 Geneva
geneva@sivananda.net
www.sivananda.ch

UNITED KINGDOM

Sivananda Yoga Vedanta Centre
45 – 51 Felsham Road
London SW15 1AZ
london@sivananda.net
www.sivanandalondon.org

UNITED STATES

Sivananda Yoga Vedanta Center
243 West 24th Street
New York, NY 10011
newyork@sivananda.org
www.sivanandanyc.org

URUGUAY

Asociación de Yoga Sivananda
Acevedo Díaz 1523
Montevideo 11200
montevideo@sivananda.org
www.sivananda.org.uy

VIETNAM

Sivananda Yoga Vedanta Centre
147/8 Nguyễn Đình Chính, Phường 11, Phú Nhuận, Hồ Chí Minh
hochiminh@sivananda.org
www.sivanandayogavietnam.org/ho-chi-minh-center

Sivananda Yoga Vedanta Centre
B2-11 Golf Valley, Ward 2,
Da Lat City, Lam Dong Province
dalat@sivananda.org
www.sivanandayogavietnam.org/sivananda-yoga-dalat-center